Dear Family Court Judge

Julie Boyd Cole
Copyright © 2018 Julie Boyd Cole

All rights reserved.

For information on receiving permission to use any portion of this publication, please email julieboydcole@gmail.com

ISBN: 1986895203
ISBN-13: 978-1986895200

DEDICATION

This work is dedicated to the more than 220 victims of domestic abuse and the children of domestic abuse who courageously answered the tough questions for this work. Their answers are within these pages, and are an open letter to all hardworking officers of the family court system and the people who rule on the custody of children.

Please honor these victims by reading their words within.

CONTENTS

	Acknowledgments	i
	Preface	1
1	Myths and Abuses in Family Court	6
2	Lost Custody	11
3	Lawyers' Advice	15
4	No Investigation of Abuse	19
5	Abuse Continues	21
6	Children of Domestic Abuse	28
7	Financial abuse using Family Court	30
8	No Trauma Treatment	32
9	No Satisfaction	34
10	Happier Stories	39
11	In Conclusion	40
	The Survey	48
	About the Author	64

ACKNOWLEDGMENTS

This work could not have be done without the assistance of the victims and those who spread the word that this study existed. I would also like to thank the experts in this field who share their work with the rest of the world.

I would like to thank social worker Jessica Goldberg and attorney Elizabeth Martin, who both work in Gainesville, FL and have helped me throughout this journey beyond my expectation. I thank them, too, for their individual efforts in helping the abused with emotional and legal support.

I would like to thank my colleague and fellow domestic abuse advocate Kristin Paul of Purple Ribbon Publishing.

I would like to thank Peaceful Paths of Gainesville, FL and their staff and donors who help abuse victims every day.

I would like to thank my editor Eileen Spiegler.

98% of responders were women abused by men.

PREFACE

"My ex-husband has used the divorce as a playground for abuse."
— a responder to a 2015-17 survey of victims of domestic abuse who share children with their abuser.

    In 2015, I wrote a simple survey for victims of domestic abuse who also share children with their abusers. I published the survey on various websites, social media and gave it to experts in the field of domestic abuse. I asked people to answer the questions anonymously. Over the next two years, more than 200 people from 27 states, the United Kingdom, Hong Kong, Australia, Canada and New Zealand responded to the survey and continue to to do so today.
    I have been researching the dynamic of domestic abuse, also called intimate partner abuse or, more appropriately, family abuse, since 2010. The dynamic is hard to understand. As a victim of domestic violence and a journalist, I have felt compelled to study this issue. I began writing articles for my blog, bruisedwoman.com, as a way to deal with co-parenting with my abuser. I then began to write articles for divorcedmoms.com and the goodmenproject.com, two websites devoted to gender specific issues of self-improvement. After that, I wrote my first book, *How to Co-Parent with an Abusive Ex and Keep Your Sanity*, as a resource for parents who are forced to co-parent with the person who abused them. Co-parenting with an abuser is a crazy-making experience for everyone but the abuser. I had to do it from the day my children were born. First, as a married couple and while suffering from physical abuse. Then, for 13 years after I divorced him. Though divorce ended the physical abuse, it did not end his efforts to abuse me. Suddenly, the children became his leverage to gain the power and control he lost in our break-up. The children became the center of almost all his efforts to abuse me. It was more painful and traumatic than any blow I ever received by his hand.
    I got through the experience with a lot of help from friends, experts, an excellent counselor and attorney. I turned my journey and research into a quick read for other parents

forced by courts to co-parent with their abusers.

After I began publishing articles about how abusers use co-parenting as another way to control their victims, I started to receive emails from people who face the same circumstance and were looking for help. By now, I've received hundreds of emails from mostly women all over America, England, Canada, Australia and Hong Kong from women looking for advice in handling this horrible dynamic.

In 2017, I sent out another survey asking children raised by domestic abusers to answer a few questions about their experience. Some left comments they wished they could have told the judge who handled their case but for one reason or another, never got the chance. This work also gives them a voice. It is a platform to speak their minds without the restrictions of a trial, motions, a hearing, or the consequences they face from their abusers.

According to the American Bar Association (ABA), most parents who break up are able to come together peacefully to decide where the minor children will live, go to school, attend church, go to college, and so on. To avoid family court intervention, both parents must make this commitment — to make these important decisions together and in the best interest of the children. Their love of their children compels them to work together. In these cases, a judge simply signs off on the arrangement.

However, in a small percentage (about 10 to 15 percent) of divorcing parents of minor children, one parent won't work with the other parent in this way. Instead, one parent chooses to take the other parent to court to decide the custody arrangement or to reopen an existing custody order. I learned that it always takes two, consenting and committed parents to agree to work together and avoid family court intervention. It takes just one parent to force legal action. Each parent has the legal right to take unlimited court actions as long as their shared children are minors. In my case, my abuser, the man who hit me multiple times and choked me while I was pregnant, filed to reopen our custody agreement five years after our divorce was final. Our children were teenagers, one was 16, and perfectly happy and healthy and their father was a regular part of their lives. After nearly a year of motions, court appearances, false accusation and trial preparation for a custody battle that shocked and traumatized me, my accuser dropped the case and finally agreed to my settlement offers days before our trial. There were no winners, except my abuser was able to terrorize me for almost a year. Not much changed in our children's lives after that, but my abuser used the experience to threaten me repeatedly for years after that until our youngest was 18 years old. He threatened me often that he would take me back to court if I didn't give in to whatever demand he thought he was entitled, regardless of our court order. I am grateful to this day that I had an excellent attorney who calmed my nerves more than once during those years. I am also grateful that I had a very detailed court order that served as a firm boundary to my abuser's demands. My therapist was instrumental in my emotional health through it all.

Occasionally, child custody is debated in the family court system because of a "third party" such as a grandparent who wants time with a child. But, the most common reason a third party gets involved in the United States is because of unpaid child support. In those cases, the state becomes an interested party in cases of unpaid child support. There are state laws that allow state agencies to independently go after "deadbeat" parents to recoup financial aid awarded to the custodial parent by the state.

No matter who is taking whom to court, various studies have shown that family court actions can be devastating to children, even if they are not brought into court or know about the action. The stress on the family alone can cause instability in the children's daily life.

After child support cases are taken out of the equation, the ABA says that a large percentage of that small segment of divorces that involve contested custody are related to domestic abuse.

Abusers "who aggressively litigate against (the protective parents) are using family court to stalk, harass, punish and impoverish their former partners," according to the National Organization for Women. Domestic abuse expert Lundy Bancroft has spent the last 25 years working with abusive men. He is a best-selling author on the topic of abuse and now trains professionals in the dynamics of abuse.

According to Bancroft, in his article "The Batterer as a Parent":

"Making appropriate assessments, especially in custody determinations: A batterer's history of abusive behavior, and how such abuse reflects on his parenting, needs to be investigated carefully, assessing for the presence of any of the common problems described above and paying particular attention to that children may become a vehicle for continued abuse of the mother. Courts need to ensure that custody evaluators have extensive training on the multiple sources of risk to children from custody or unsupervised contact with the abusive parent."

It is clear that some abuser use civil law, family court and family court judges to further abuse their family and try to win back the power and control they once had over them. They can use co-parenting and 50/50 custody standards common today to further abuse the family. They may claim that they want to be a part of the children's lives or they feel entitled to the daily parenting of the children.

Those sentiments are supported by many family courts officials because these are often the sentiments of loving, involved parents. However, two good parents rarely need family court to sort out their parenting differences. In practice, abusers don't know how to be good parents and don't see the damage such strife does to their children, nor do they really care. An abuser ultimately wants control of the family in order to exploit them when they need to feel better about themselves, and they use family court judges and custody laws to do so. The simple act of battling in court gives many abusers the rush they seek. The outcome of fight doesn't always matter to an abuser.

When it does, control over other people is the goal. Controlling others is a antidote that calms their anxiety, their insecurity, their broken egos and personality disorders.

The New York State Office for the Prevention of Domestic Violence turned to Evan Stark, Ph.D. MSW, a forensic social worker and professor emeritus at Rutgers University, to explain coercive control. He said:

> "Domestic violence comprises a range of behaviors beyond physical and emotional abuse. Abusers often use violence, intimidation, degradation and isolation to deprive victims of their rights to physical security, dignity and respect. Evan Stark has been encouraging the use of 'coercive control' to describe a course of oppressive behavior grounded in gender-based privilege. <u>While all forms of abuse are about power and control, coercive control is a strategic form of ongoing oppression and terrorism</u> that invades all arenas of women's activity by limiting access to money and other basic resources. In addition, few elements of coercive control are currently considered criminal, or are only crimes when committed against strangers, which further complicates this issue within the context of domestic violence.
>
> "Coercive control is a strategic course of oppressive behavior designed to secure and expand gender-based privilege by depriving women of their rights and liberties and establishing a regime of domination in personal life. This definition reminds us that women are often targets of violence. I wrote Coercive Control (Oxford, 2007) to examine the oppressive tactics some males used to dominate women.
>
> "Coercive control refers to abuse as a 'strategic course of oppressive behavior,'

meaning that battering is: rational, instrumental behavior and not a loss of control; 'ongoing' rather than episodic; based on multiple tactics like violence, intimidation, degradation, isolation and control.

"Sixty to 80 percent of abused women experience coercive control beyond physical and emotional abuse.

"Men possess 'gender-based privilege' because they are male. While all forms of abuse are about 'power and control,' women are vulnerable to coercive control because of unequal political status and because men can take advantage of pervasive sexual inequalities in ways women cannot. While control involves everything from survival resources like money, to what television shows women watch, male abusers exploit and regulate women's sexuality (e.g., how they dress, wear their hair, make love, etc.) and how they perform traditional gender roles as housewives and mothers.

"Coercive control is a violation of 'rights and liberties' protected by the U.S. Constitution and international human rights conventions, including right to physical security (violence); to live without fear (intimidation); to dignity and respect (degradation); to social intercourse (isolation) and to autonomy, liberty and personhood (control). Over time, victimization and dependence are replaced by domination/subordination, agency and resistance. Emphasis shifts from what men do to women to what they keep women from doing."

Forced co-parenting with an abuser throws victims of domestic abuse back into a pseudo-relationship with their abuser. Only now, the abuser can legally abuse the former partner by using the children as objects of debate in indirect attacks to hurt their victims. The laws in many countries and states do not limit the number of motions and court actions any parent can file against the other until their youngest child reaches the age of 18. Abusers are often without a conscience, or the judgment non-abusers find holds them back from using family court to settle parenting disputes.

Most parents believe that a lawsuit over custody and parenting decisions is too disruptive to their children's lives, so those who put their children first try hard to avoid legal action. They try hard to treat their children as people, not the property at the center of a civil suit. Unfortunately, it takes only one parent to files a lawsuit. That parent is the plaintiff and the other, often abuse victim, becomes the defendant.

Abusers don't go to the court as a way to "work things out." They go to court as a way to terrorize their victims.

In 2017, my anonymous survey of people who were at the center of one or more custody actions filed by one parent against another showed what the scientific studies are finding: domestic abusers are using family court as a way to continue to abuse; abusers use family court to gain control over their victims; abusers are using parenting rights as a right to abuse their families; victims are suffering with little support or recourse to end the abuse; and court officials are not trained in this particular type of domestic abuse. Most court officials do not have much experience with this type of domestic abuse since dockets are populated most with uncontested child custody arrangements connected to divorce or child support cases.

However, depending on which study or state is examined, between 25 and 50 percent of all family court domestic relationship actions are reopened cases, indicating that one person in the former union is pursuing court intervention for a second, third, or more times. This is an effective way to harm the other parent, by creating economic hardships in legal fees, job disruption, instability and more.

An abuser can recreate the most important factor to gain back power — fear. Legal action creates enormous uncertainty in the defendants' and the children's lives. Many abusers enjoy the power they feel once again and the control over their adversaries — their exes. Children who live in such an unstable environment have been shown to have lifelong negative effects as a result, according to the U.S. Centers for Disease Control. Statistically, family court does not help children, and may in fact, further hurt children and victims of domestic abuse.

This book includes the direct comments submitted by the victims of domestic abuse and their children. The respondents submitted comments anonymously, answering 32 questions about their experience. They had nothing to gain by answering the survey, except maybe, finally having the opportunity to share how they feel about the abuse as a result of family court.

On the following pages are their comments and some of the results of multiple choice questions. The comments have been only slightly edited for clarity. Otherwise, they are taken directly from the survey responses.

For further information about these two surveys, please contact Julie Boyd Cole at julieboydcole@gmail.com.

57% of responders said the domestic abuse was not presented in their custody case.

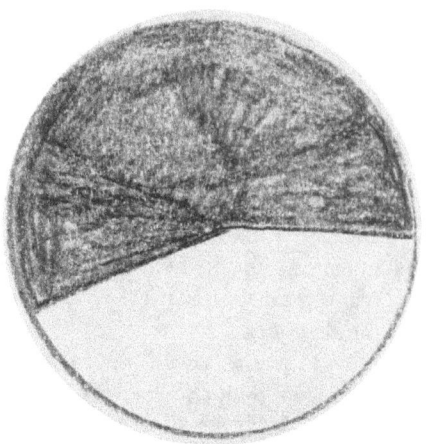

CHAPTER 1
MYTHS AND ABUSES IN FAMILY COURT

Myth: "The system is set up to help you."
Myth: "Courts protect children from abusers."
— the National Organization for Women, which found the the opposite to be true.

Myth: "Mothers frequently invent allegations of child sexual abuse to win custody.
— 2006 finding by the American Bar Association Commission on Domestic Violence, which found the opposite to be true.

According to the American Bar Association: "Child sexual abuse allegations in custody cases are rare (about 6 percent), and the majority of allegations are substantiated (⅔)."
– *Thoennes & Tjaden, The Extent, Nature, And Validity of Sexual Abuse Allegations in Custody And Visitation Disputes, 14(2) Child Sexual Abuse & Neglect 151-63 (1900).*

"False allegations are no more common in divorce or custody disputes than at any other time."
– *Brown, Frederico, Hewitt, & Sheehan, Revealing The Existence of Child Abuse in the Context of Marital Breakdown And Custody and Access Disputes, 24(6) Child Abuse & Neglect 849-85 (2000).*

"Among false allegations, fathers are far more likely than mothers to make intentionally false accusation (21% compared to 1.3%)."
– *Bala & Schuman, Allegations of Sexual Abuse When Parents Have Separated, 17 Canadian Family Law*

Quarterly 191-241 (2000).

In the 2015-17 survey for this book of adult and minor children who were the center of a child custody case, the following results revealed:

- When the children were asked to list the people in the court process they trusted, 0 percent said they trusted the judge or the parent coordinator assigned their case;

- 47 percent of the children in the custody cases said they specifically didn't trust the judge and 53 percent said they didn't trust the attorneys involved;

- 87 percent said they experienced high levels of stress before the case;

- 93 percent of the children said they experienced high levels of stress after the case closed;

- 88 percent said that family court needs reform;

- Only 19 percent of the children of the custody disputes were happy with the outcome of their custody case;

- Only 19 percent felt their wishes and voices were considered in the case;

- 82 percent of the children said that domestic abuse was in the home before the case;

- 76 percent said their abusive parent traumatized them during their childhood;

- 76 percent said their abusive parent physically assaulted them;

- Only 7 percent of the responders said that the abuse stopped after the custody case, and only 7 percent said their home life was more stable after the case than before, and in those cases, it was because they were protected from the abusers.

This anonymous survey suggests that the family court is not working to help stabilize the lives of children of a volatile union after the break-up of their parents.

Though there are many studies in institutions around the world that shows why family court on the whole is damaging to children and victims of domestic abuse, I thought it best to let the children and adult children of contested custody cases speak for themselves. Here is what they said:

> **"I would like (the court authorities) to know that even though they tried to break me and keep me away from my mom, they lost and I am happier than ever with my loving parent who should have had custody all along,"** wrote a 17-year-old girl.

> From a 42-year-old man who was the subject of a custody case when he was a child: **"My dad knows what he did. My mom and I paid the price of his hatred and never ending litigation and over 16 false CPS** (Child Protective Services) **reports. They are worthless, too."**

From a 14-year-old boy:
"If there is a restraining order against a parent, it is for a good reason. That parent tortured me and punished me and pushed me to punish my mother; and alienated me from my mother; then moved me into his girlfriend's house. My mother always put my needs first. My father always saw me as invisible and made me suffer. I think he only took me to punish my mom for the restraining order and encouraged me to be mean to my mom. My mom was the most important person in my life and hurting her, as he made me do, hurt me so deeply I spent a month in a mental hospital."

From a 32-year-old woman who was the subject of a child custody case:
"They knowingly sent me and my brother to live with the man they knew was beating us and regularly threatened to kill us. They should be ashamed of themselves and I consider those family court actors to be responsible for every beating my brother and I received after that decision was made."

From an 18-year-old woman that was a subject of a child custody case:
"The issues and solutions aren't always black and white."

From a 16-year-old boy:
"It is extremely important that children have a voice. Age and maturity are important but when older siblings are involved they should be able to help speak for the younger. Guardian ad litems need to be appointed and used. If children want to speak to judges they should have the opportunity."

From a 38-year-old woman who was the subject of a child custody case:
"Other family members were coerced by my father into lying on the stand. In fact, a sibling was promised and later given as a reward a brand new car if she would lie on the stand. Their decision to send me to my father subjected me to further abuses. To this day, I'm nearly 40, my father is still verbally and emotionally abusive and I have no contact with him. They were played like fiddles by him and I will never forgive him or them."

From an 8-year-old boy:
"They should have listened to me. I didn't want to have 50-50."

From an 18-year-old woman who was the subject of a child custody case:
"The legal professionals are unable to see the whole picture, beneath the surface. This complicates how the suitable guardian is chosen. Much of violence by women is also overlooked in family court and not pursued criminally."

From a 19-year-old man who was the subject of a child custody case:
"Figure out how to ID and penalize abusers early on so that fewer kids have to live through what I did."

From a 42-year-old man who was the subject of a child custody dispute when he was a child:
"My dad should be ASHAMED. I was just a pawn to hurt my mom. My mom

is my bff."

From an 18-year-old woman who was the subject of a child custody dispute when she was a child:
"The child should have a say."

From a 14-year-old boy:
"The custody split me in half. My father had me five days then I went back to my mother for two then back to him, then back to her. It was crazy. I was never ever allowed to spend Christmas with my own relatives; but had to be at all his girlfriend's functions. It is hard being ignored by your own father while he dotes on his girlfriend's children."

From a 37-year-old woman who was the subject of a child custody dispute when she was a child:
"They made a mistake in placing us with our mother; she was an addict and unstable. It affects me still today."

From an 18-year-old woman who was the subject of a child custody dispute when she was a child:
"They did the best they could."

From an 18-year-old woman who was the subject of a child custody dispute:
"I'm not property. Listen to the abused parent!"

In the 2015-2017 survey of a former partner co-parenting with their abuser mentioned in the Preface, only 14 percent of the 204 respondents said they felt they were fairly treated by the family court system, and only 20 percent were satisfied with the result of the case. Ninety-four percent think the family court system needs reform. Again, I think it is best to let the responders speak for themselves:

From a mother in the United States:
"There is a massive disconnect in family court regarding violent men and their ability/willingness to 'parent,' 'co-parent'/cooperate in a non-abusive manner. Just because you are no longer together doesn't mean they are no longer batterers and there is a false belief that a violent man can be a good parent. 'Good fathers don't abuse their children's mother,' said Lundy Bancroft the author and expert in domestic violence. The statistics are very clear that batterers are likely to expose the children to more domestic violence (new relationship), abuse the children and continue to abuse the children's mother. There are also little to no resources to help children and mothers deal with continued abuse through court ordered contact in the name of 'fairness'."

From a mother in the United Kingdom:
"The abuse was very covert and the furthest things went was mediation, then he stopped attending after two sessions. I have parental responsibility and our child lives with me."

From another mother in the United States:

"The courts operate using the 'fact' that all children are better off if they are involved with both parents.

"The courts refuse to understand that an abusive person doesn't just abuse one person. They refuse to understand, refuse to care, that the victim will continue to be abused, and that the child will be in direct line of abuse, quite simply because they are the child of the mother and because they are vulnerable. They will wait for the bruises to appear before they act. In regards to mental abuse, they simply do not care.

"I never could have imagined the additional trauma caused by the broken family court system and the way it empowers abusers. I feel more frightened and more broken now, four years after I got out."

7% of responders said their abusers have custody of their kids 70% to 100% of the time; 25% said their abusers have custody 50% of the time; and 19% said their abuser have custody 30% of the time in any given month.

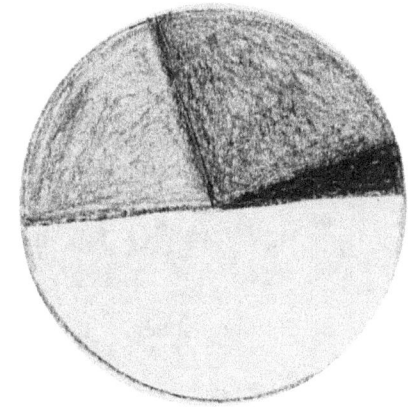

CHAPTER 2
LOST CUSTODY

As unthinkable as it seems, there are many cases in which the abusers, even rapists and sex abusers, have won full custody of their children from the arms of the victims, the protective parents. Some protective parents are so anxious about family court and the potential outcome for their children, that they come across as uncooperative or crazed. Family court judges can misread them as the problem. Some protective parents have lost custody of their children because the family court believed their abusers' deceptions that the other parent is lying about the abuse or that abuse is not relevant. Some judges don't believe that domestic abuse between the parents is a sound reason to deny custody to the abuser. While other judges simple don't have the court time to unravel the domestic mess before it.

All of these factors play into the hands of the abusers, because ultimately, they don't have anything to lose in family court. If they lose custody, they enjoyed wreaking havoc on their victims for as long as it lasted and they generally don't care how it affected their children. They are emboldened by the battle, especially since there are rarely consequences, and may even be planning their next legal assault. If they win any form of parenting rights or custody, they have won the control of another human beings for as long as the children are minors, sometimes even longer. They can also use the children to create fear in their exes.

Court officials often don't focus on the big picture _ what is best for the children _ and work the immediate problem before it instead. Some don't see it as their role to set up a family situation that will best protect the children from abuse by a parent or protect the victim from further domestic abuse. It is hard to understand why so many judges, attorneys and court officials ignore the obvious. Abuser do not make good parents, or even goodenough parents. Abusers do not make good co-parenting partners either. Abusers can't ever be trusted.

The Centers for Disease Control found in the Adverse Childhood Experiences (ACE) study that childhood traumas, such as those caused by these dynamics, have a long-lasting, negative effect. Children who are raised by abusers or even by a parent, who is being terrorized by an abuser, face a high chance of permanent emotional, mental, developmental and physical challenges, diseases and disorders. The cost of treating all of this has been estimated by some experts as an expense of billions of dollars every year.

It is clear, family abuse is deeply relevant in child custody.

Again, I turn to the words of the respondents of the 2015-2017 survey of parents who share children with their abusers. They said:

> "I'm toward the end of this 10-year nightmare. [My ex-husband] successfully gained custody of our older child, our son, through abuse and manipulation through the court system. He abused him for three and a half years. At 9 a.m. on the morning of my son's 18th birthday, he kicked him out on the streets. After three and half years of despicable things being said about me and my husband, my son refused to come home and is currently in the struggle of a lifetime — spiraling downward, and fast. I am currently happy with the custody agreement with our youngest, our daughter, as she only has to visit one weekend a month and half of school breaks. I have since cut off all phone and text contact with my ex. I will only communicate via email. And unless it is something I deem important, I do not respond. Because most of his emails are intended to abuse and intimidate. I don't respond often."

> "My ex lied to the court and made my children fear me and my house by saying it was haunted and I was a witch. After I had custody, he took me back [to court] for custody and had my oldest, 8-year-old daughter lie that I was abusive and she wanted to live with her father. She is now 23 and we still don't have a relationship, but I fear the relationship with her father is incestuous. I have given up trying to help her."

> "It is horrible that our legal system forces young children to spend so much time, unsupervised, with abusers. Mine is an active alcoholic with an explosive temper who was diagnosed with narcissistic personality disorder and who cheated on me with prostitutes. I pray every day for my child's protection."

> "My ex threatened during the marriage if I ever left he would take my children. He successfully did this from the moment he received the papers I filed. Originally, I filed for legal separation and that both parties go to therapy. He then re-filed for a bifurcated divorce. Meanwhile, he was hiding my daughter, and to this day, nine years later, I still do not see her. She is scared to death of me because of the lies he tells."

> "Children get put in dangerous and life-altering situations because the COURTS DON'T GET IT."

"I would prefer I had full custody but most likely not happening due to my being unemployed. I may go back in the future to fight for it depending on what I hear from my 11-year-old during her time with him and me finding employment."

"My divorce from my ex-husband took place 12 years ago. One of my children is now 19 and living with her boyfriend. My two other children with him are now 13 and 16. They live with their dad because they have behavior problems and disabilities, and I am unable to handle them. I get them on weekends, but it is a challenge because my 13-year-old is so mean to my 8-year-old daughter, and I am afraid he will hurt her. He looks and acts so much like his father. I am afraid that he will seriously hurt someone, or get hurt himself. I fear that he will end up in jail, and it breaks my heart because he can be such a sweet kid. I have been in another abusive marriage since that time, but am now divorced. I still suffer from the trauma and don't know how to trust anyone. I have sought counseling, studied, and have a great support network, but never seem to get completely free of my past hurts."

"To this day no one believes that he ever abused me at all. I lost my children, my husband, my home, my vehicle, my extended family, all friends, daughter's friends and their parents, daughter's school, almost everyone but my mom. But she passed in 2013. Most days it is hard to find hope as my daughter is now 17, she has untreated anxiety and depression, and does not want contact with me at all. My son (24) is the same way. I find hope (some) and a lot of resolve working with my therapist. Does my partial story ring any bells for a support group?"

"My ex now uses the court system what seems like every day. He has custody of one of my children and even this past weekend called the police on me for trying to pick up my child. He was not going to let me have him unless I told him I would do things that I didn't want to do. He even went as far as telling me I will have consequences for what he thinks are unfavorable choices. I can't get rid of him, the less I talk to him, the worst he gets. And now that he has custody of one of my children, I feel like I will only get peace if I lose my children."

"My ex-husband dragged our divorce into a custody battle, used techniques of parental alienation to manipulate my daughter. The divorce took SIX YEARS. He convinced her to lie to the forensic psychologist, etc. She became a basket case, to the point where she was cutting, restricting her food and passing out. She became increasingly anxious and depressed and was almost hospitalized — he refused to allow her to be hospitalized. I've had her in therapy since the week I left him. Therapy could not counteract what he was doing to her. I finally voluntarily gave him physical custody so that his emotional abuse of her would stop, and so he could 'win.' She is now 17. My daughter and I are very close but she still lives with her chronically unemployed father, has been involved with drugs, drinking, started having sex at 14, smokes, failed school every year since he got custody of her. He is still holding her emotionally hostage by telling her he cannot survive without my child support, and if she leaves, he as 'no one.' Apparently, he has a gambling problem now. This was the man the COURT APPOINTED FORENSIC PSYCHOLOGIST RECOMMENDED GET CUSTODY OF MY CHILD. I didn't lie enough, apparently, to be a good enough mother. The court system is broken; whomever has the most money (or is willing to go bankrupt in order to win), is willing to lie the most, and destroy the children in the process, can 'win' custody. My former divorce attorney will actually no longer take custody cases!"

"My judge is corrupt. My abusive ex has temporary custody of my daughter when I have had custody of her whole life and have two gals that report that I should have sole custody. The judge ignored all my evidence."

"I think I could write a book from what I need to say. I really want to help other mothers to never go through what I have been through, although I hear it is fairly common. I said at the time of court that it was the 'ole boy network' that make the decision for my son to live with his dad. My female attorney, whom I found at the local domestic violence place, really was pretty slack, as well."

"Family court is corrupt. They ignore any evidence brought forward by the victim, including police videos and recordings of children disclosing sexual abuse. Full custody and full parental rights were given to the perpetrator of the abuse."

16% of responders said their attorney told them not to introduce the domestic abuse into the custody case; 16% said they didn't have a chance to because they filed a no-fault divorce; 6% didn't introduce the domestic abuse into the case because they didn't think they needed to.

CHAPTER 3
LAWYERS' ADVICE

Many victims of domestic abuse have a hard time paying for good legal representatives. Abusers tend to be the partner in power, and often the partner with the most money between the two. Many communities in the United States do not have any attorneys who specialize in representing in family court victims of abuse. Further, it is common for attorneys to advise protective parents to stay silent about the domestic abuse while before family court judges. Many attorney's worry that their case can be upended by an allegation of abuse made by their client because they fear the judge will assume it is made up to gain advantage. It is also common legal advice in family court today that protective parents should never curtail any visitation between their abuser and the child no matter how much they fear for their safety. Victims are often told never to even worry about it out loud to a family court official, because it might paint them as a hyper-vigilant parent unwilling to co-parent or a liar.

On this topic, here are some of the comments from the responders of the survey regarding their experiences with their lawyers:

> "My attorney told me if I went for supervised visitation, it would take at least a half-day of court time and I couldn't afford it."

> "My lawyers have consistently told me not to bring up the fact that my child, at age 5, made an outcry to me about playing with his dad's penis, which I reported to CPS; or that my child told me more recently that his dad showed

him a video of a young girl's genitalia, which my lawyers advised me not to report to CPS. To do so would have endangered my case and make me look like an alienator, and I could lose even more time with my child. Repeatedly, I was advised not to bring up abuse issues. However, my ex did bring up my report to CPS and the fact that CPS 'ruled out' the abuse to accuse me of 'parental alienation.' "

"My lawyers fought for me every single day. My first lawyer started down the collaborative path without telling me. It was a disaster. There should be no collaborative divorce when there is an abusive situation. Every problem and mistake I am still dealing with came from that part of the process. I got very lucky that my ex is well-known and did not want to submit to a custody evaluation, but he has made life extremely difficult for me. Also, I have a better custody arrangement than many women in similar circumstances. I had to do that by moving out of my home in two hours, with the police, and taking my kids. It was a nightmare. And very destructive to the kids to have to do a 'SWAT' move. From family photos to my grandmother's items, I had to leave many things behind forever."

"My divorce cost me a fortune in terms of what I didn't fight for and what I agreed to pay my ex. I was willing to do anything to get out of that marriage. The legal system failed me because attorneys told me to 'get over it.' Eleven years later, and I'm still paying for those financial mistakes."

"Attorneys don't get it, and they don't care to get it."

"The law to date is imperfect to say the least. What should be concerning is what the law is teaching our children with the mishandling of divorce cases complicated by domestic violence. Without continued physical assault, a lawyer may portray the victim as the abuser in her failure to leave the abuser when opportunity presents itself. If you get out, don't even look back or you will suffer forever and might as well be dead. You won't matter anymore except to your abuser, who will put the mighty cuckold of pure control of your every breath forever, without reprieve, as mandated by lawyer in divorce court of law."

"Ex's barrister and lawyers added in things to the court order that judge didn't order after court. They had the order sealed without showing me for approval and I received it two weeks later. The courts have never asked me to submit statements to show his lies. I act alone, ex is wealthy and has a good legal team and barristers."

"The lawyers not only failed to present the evidence of domestic abuse, they were insensitive and dismissive about my history as domestic abuse victim, asking victim-blaming questions. One even said the problem of the abuse and conflict is due to 'cultural differences' — and she is supposed to be a very experienced family lawyer. The judge, who simply described the marriage as 'turbulent,' only paid attention after I kept pushing my lawyers to highlight the issue in my affirmations and the summons."

"My ex's attorney went to school with the judge and there was a blatant bias in the courtroom."

"I don't feel my attorney or the courts realize how they affect and control the future of an individual. My attorney said in a few years my ex would move on to another job and said I would be able to move. Thirteen years later, here I am. I will have to stay another eight to reach retirement before I move away from my ex and begin the life I would like to live. By then, my entire youth will be behind me."

"I BEG the court system to recognize this disorder and help ex-spouses find relief from having to co-parent with them. PLEASE EDUCATE THE JUDGES AND ATTORNEYS."

"Domestic violence education should be a requirement for all legal professionals. There are many situations that have flown low under the radar and been dismissed as a civil issues."

"I have an attorney but it makes no difference."

"Little recognition of the impact of emotional abuse, coercion, manipulation. Cluster B personality disorders are not understood by judges and lawyers."

"The court system, judges, mediators, attorneys and all others involved in divorce need to go through training about all facets of abuse. How the abuser will manipulate the situation to benefit them and only them."

"Courts should take abuse into consideration more than they do. Attorneys don't want to mention it because of the stigma of domestic violence. Find an experienced attorney that's not afraid to speak your truth."

"I am currently proposing my daughter (age 15) be in charge of when she wants to see her dad. She doesn't want to do any overnights with him. She has come to terms with his emotional abuse of her when she is with him. My lawyer advised that for calculating child support we say she will be with him one three-day weekend a month but that she is allowed to refuse. He is going to get very mad and I am worried what he will do to me. The woman he cheated on me with contacted me to tell me he raped and beat her and she realized he's a narcissist (he raped me toward the end of our marriage). She said he had talked about suicide with her several times and that he had smuggled his late father's unregistered guns into Canada. He told her he wanted to 'off' me so he wouldn't have to pay spousal support. The police wouldn't take a report because it was a third party threat and my lawyer said I couldn't get a restraining order based on her word. Our parenting plan change hearing is on January 5. My son is 20 so he isn't involved in custody, but lives with me full-time as well with the occasional visit to see his dad. My son has Asperger's and my ex was much more abusive to him emotionally and physically but never left marks for me to have proof. He threw my son around. Once he threw a cup of coffee on him when my son was 1. My son sadly is dying for his dad's approval and doesn't think his dad was or is abusive."

"I am in battle now with my abuser and having to fight pro se after he filed outlandish emergency hearing and full custody of kids and has found me in contempt because kids do not call him every second of the day they are home, literally."

"I was married to my ex for almost seven years. The only reason it lasted that long was the fact he was deployed for half of it. He was emotionally, financially, and sexually abusive. I had one foot out the door when I learned I was pregnant. Two years went by and things got worse. He threatened me when he came home on leave and I knew that it was time to leave because I knew he was going to get physical. When we separated, he came back to the house one night and tried to break down the bedroom door. Stupid me, I didn't call the cops but filed for an EPO and divorce the next day. At the advice of my lawyer, I didn't pursue DVO. I regret not pursuing psych evaluation on him because I feel that things would be different. We believe he has borderline personality disorder."

"My ex-husband and I actually get along pretty well for the kids, and have always tried to put the kids first, but I know that my kids have been affected by the divorce, changes in living situations, and being in the middle of a sad situation. I think many victims agree to custody agreements because of fear and intimidation, and there is not a lot of support. I feel guilty that I don't have my boys living with me, and that I have to have their dad help, especially since I don't feel that he is the best role model, but I feel helpless. He's the only other person responsible for them. I know that my son is taking after his father and I fear that he will become an abuser."

"Each person should be counseled individually in mediation, then together. My case went to court and I got the notice after it was over and he went to court with his lawyer. Should not have been allowed to go without me."

26% of responders said the domestic abuse they reported to authorities was investigated.

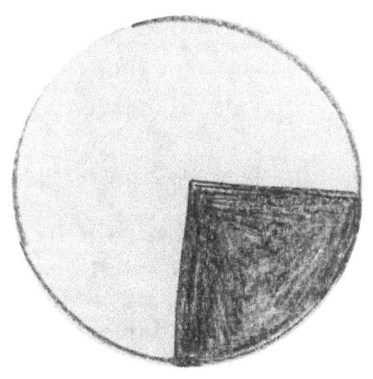

CHAPTER 4
NO INVESTIGATION OF ABUSE

Domestic abuse is one of the most unreported, common crimes in the United States. Every minute, 20 people are physically assaulted by an intimate partner in the United States, according to the National Coalition Against Domestic Violence. The NCADV also found that the vast majority of domestic abuse cases _ 75 percent _ go unreported to the police. According to the Washington, D.C. Coalition Against Domestic Violence, one of the reasons why these crimes are not reported by the victims, most of whom are women, is because they believe that the police will do nothing about it.

Even with the high level of under-reporting, in the District of Columbia, for example, domestic violence still accounts for half of all violent crimes reported.

Rather than report the crime of domestic abuse, victims are more likely to leave the relationship. Victims often falsely believing that the abuse was the result of a dysfunctional union rather than because they were in the life of an abuser. Leaving an abuser dramatically increases the chance of further abuse, the national organization found. The NCADV also found that a victim of abuse endure 35 assaults on average before they finally make their first police report.

These statistics show what so many responders of the survey for this book told, that abuse by an intimate partner is not a matter the authorities really want to tackle. In my case, I ignorantly believed that my most responsible move was to leave my abuser. I believed that would end the abuse and make everyone lives, including my children's, better. I didn't realized that the abuse was the result of an abuser's actions and his need to have power and control over others. That need doesn't go away after divorce. My children and I will always be in the orbit of an abuser. Leaving was indeed a responsible and important choice to protect myself and my children, but it was by no means the stopgap to his abuse. Family court was just one way I was and other victims are further abused.

In family court, which is a civil court, there are few mechanisms to investigated abuse , including criminal abuse, reported during divorce and custody actions. Too often, the court assumes the abuse has been investigated by other agencies, when it has not. Further, victims may use the divorce as a way to end the abuse rather than filing criminal charges. This leads to incorrect assumptions that when the history of abuse is revealed in family court, it is either irrelevant, unrelated or a ploy to gain advantage.

In this survey, very few respondents said the abuse they offered as evidence in family court was ever investigated by any authority. Here are the voices of the victims who responded to the survey:

> "Emotional abuse is virtually impossible to substantiate in court."

> "Where are the program's monitoring child-parent relationships during and after orders of protection are issued? We need structured transitions for allowing children access to parents after domestic violence has occurred based on a team approach including counselors, parents, law guardians, etc. It seems that there is nothing out there."

> "I brought a modification for Soberlink alcohol monitoring, after he left our child in a hot car when buying booze; after he had been seen at school drunk when he was going to be driving our child. It took the court more than one year and five hearings, costing me attorneys' fees of $75,000, before the judge would authorize me to be able to pick up my child when his dad failed Soberlink."

> "The court ignores threats, harassment and bullying. Even to extended family."

86% of responders said they are still being abused by their former partner, through co-parenting.

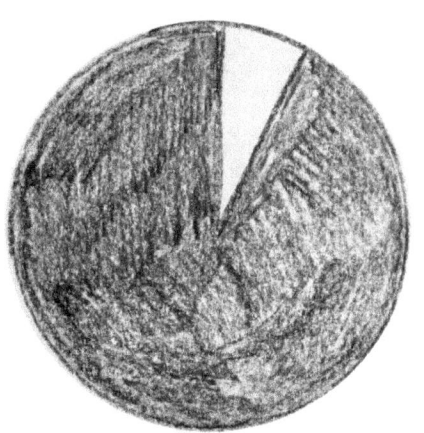

CHAPTER 5
ABUSE CONTINUES

"Women are most vulnerable to violence when separated from their intimate partner. The second most vulnerable group are those who are divorced. This can discourage women from leaving their abusive partner, out of fear that it will increase their risk of victimization."
– DC Coalition Against Domestic Violence

Abusers hurt their family members for their own reasons. Plenty of people get mad at others or say things they regret, but abusers cause pain in order to feel powerful and in control and to quiet their inner, self-disparaging voice. When abusers dominate another human being, they feel like they are winning an important fight, and that makes them feel good.

However, in most daily relationships — with co-workers, neighbors, strangers on the bus — there are negative consequences for abusive behavior, sometimes very serious consequences that can act as deterrent for the abuser. They aren't looking for a real fight, after all, just the feeling of power. Think of a bully in the schoolyard. Divorce doesn't cure an abuser's need to cause hurt and fear, it just changes the availability to what had been an easy and accessible target, their intimate partner and children. Domestic abusers find ways to continue involvement with anyone they can repeatedly use and exploit. Statistically, they rarely will let that victim go without a fight, or many fights. If there are children involved, and family court, abusers have essentially free reign to intimate and bully those victims again and again.

An abuser's family provides a unique and repeated opportunity to exploit, like a fly in a spider's web.

When a victim leaves, the abuser often tries to win back their victims by wooing them back with promises of change. Others try to stop their victims from leaving with threats. And others move on to other partners and start the dynamic all over again. But, according to domestic violence expert Lundy Bandcroft, they never learn to stop. And they never lose the need.

This puts all family members of an abuser in harm's way for the rest of the abuser's life, and is why they are most life-threatening after the victim has ended the relationship. Sometimes, they feel like they have nothing else to lose, so they strike the hardest.

Children and family court provide a new path for abusers. Not only are victims in most danger after they leave their abusers, but so are their children. Co-parenting puts both partners and children in the direct line of the abuser to use the legal system for coercive control methods, including financial, emotional and physical abuse.

The experiences of the more than 200 victims who answered the survey for this book weighed in on this as well:

> "I am abused on a daily basis trying to co-parent. He demeans me every day. I feel trapped and I can't get out because I am required by the court to communicate with him. He knows no one cares because no one stops him. The judges and attorneys hate to hear about parents fighting. They think it's petty and not abusive. It is constant abuse and keeps me from being the best mother that I can be because it erodes at my self-esteem and makes me feel worthless and helpless."

> "Sharing custody with your abuser gives them power to abuse more ... In an even more painful way, using your child."

> "My ex-husband is a cop, and I can't get help. He knows the judges and I showed up to a courtroom of uniformed officers who don't know my children. He hit me two days ago when I tried to stop him from leaving with my children in a rage. Despite my efforts to stop him, the police let him leave with my children. The police denied me the right to press charges. They said I caused it because I reached into his car for my crying son. I am all bruised up, and he gets to walk. Of course, it's my fault! He claimed I put 'his' daughter in danger and forced my way into his vehicle. I'm living in hell. Every move I make he puts me down, threatens me and terrorizes my children. I don't know who to turn to. I can't call the police, my lawyer [is terrible]. I'm tired of fighting every day just to be my children's mother."

> "I want my children to have a relationship with their dad in some way. How do you encourage a relationship with someone you are afraid of?"

> "My former spouse filed multiple motions against me after the divorce. I spent over $75,000 in legal fees and ended up having to go through mediation on my own. I lost a job because of the time and stress involved on top of single parenting (he lives out of state with no address on file) our two children."

> "My children are now grown. It was a complete and utter nightmare for 18 years. He still lies, still manipulates. He is crazy and psychotic. Took years of recovery for me. I hurt for my kids they didn't have normal father or life."

> "Never married. Filed child support temporarily. Afraid to file again. I don't want the abuser to have rights to the child. He still tries to contact me and

threatens me. Even when he is in prison in another state. Has never paid child support or visited the child. I live in fear that he would. I need help."

"I am trying to change my son's school and schedule and he refuses to change and is nitpicking the child support. He doesn't feel that I am entitled to anything. He changed the locks on our house and refused to divide up items when I moved out."

"I received permission to move away to another state. Three years after the restraining order expired, he moved to the state I was in, about 2 miles away. He went back to court for more custody but was basically denied. However, a new parenting plan was developed since the kids were older and now in the same state. He doesn't follow any of the order and causes problems with every little part of it and continues to take me to court. I don't know why the judges can't see the past abuse, bullying, control and harassment. It just continues through the court. Nothing seems to be done about it. I keep to myself and let the lawyers handle. It is sick that I am spending all my money on keeping a sociopath away from me. I am happy with my boys who know the truth, a good husband, who treats me well, and blessed baby."

"It's impossible to prove emotional abuse to a court. My ex was emotionally abusive to me, and a few times physically abusive. He blames me for everything. He is always gone and I take care of our children for months at a time without him. Yet he is still fighting my case to amend our 50/50 custody agreement. He sends me abusive texts and blames me for not catering to him."

"I am still suffering PTSD from years of emotional abuse in the marriage and the traumatic events of the divorce. I am always waiting for the other shoe to drop and wondering what I'm going to read in the next email _ demands, declarations, accusations?"

"My ex is extremely smart. He never says or does anything in public that would make him look bad. Even during our marriage he wasn't super obvious about his emotional abuse. It took me years to see that I was so unhappy with him but didn't know why. Once we had children it became clear. I was tolerating mean things said to me but could see it clearly once I was a mother. I realized I would never let him say those things to our children. Still, I didn't leave until I took a job three hours away and he admitted he was cheating."

"Because of the current domestic abuse charge, I have full legal sole custody. He has visitation, which he didn't exercise for nine months. He currently, habitually, changes his availability for visitation, has canceled and has yet to have an overnight visit."

"My ex is threatening to take me back to court for more time with our child. He had to complete 10 sessions of psychotherapy to get unsupervised access to our child. Since then he has continually bullied me and threatening court to get more time. He sent a letter with lies and manipulation and I just don't trust the psychotherapy worked at all. I am scared of going back to court and don't believe they will protect our child again, now that my ex has done as they asked. His behavior has not changed and I am so scared that I can't protect her if the court decides to give overnights. He is an alcoholic, and abusive and very manipulative. He won't tell me where he is living or where he plans to take our daughter."

"Without proper finances, I cannot afford counseling and attorney fees to protect myself in court. I am forced to live in a state 11 hours away from all family. I am not allowed to move without going to court. I have lived in the town my ex wanted to live in for the last 13 years since our divorce. It will be four more years until my kids graduate. I am trapped in every way!"

"I mediated a temporary agreement one month ago after being served approximately 20 times over the last two years, since the birth of my child. I have been in court numerous times, including seven weeks after the birth of my baby via C-section to adjudicate paternity, even though the father was present at all doctor's appointments and the hospital the day our son was born. The father of my child moved in with a nurse from the hospital to try and gain full custody. She harassed and stalked me, too, and claimed to be my child's mother."

"I have been divorced for 15 years, but my ex has managed to be persuasive enough people to convince my children that the abuse I suffered for years was all in my head and an overreaction to the circumstances. He has involved my brother and sister-in-law in perpetuating these lies. I now have no relationship with any of them. Though I endured the trauma of divorcing him, his abuse is allowed to continue by poisoning my family relationships. Thank you for exploring this topic of abuse."

"Been apart five years and I am still being bullied. He has been unemployed more than once and I am currently receiving zero in support. When he is employed, he makes well over $100,000."

"Typical, an abuser who has financial resources (his family) continues to project onto me what he is guilty of. I am going bankrupt as he continues to abuse me through the court. He tried to sabotage my parenting my child by parent alienation, vexatious litigation, and abusing our child with lies and guilt and not letting her connect with me on the phone, ever."

"He is allowed to continue to mentally and emotionally abuse me because he has money, even though I have full legal and physical custody of the children."

"Even though I filed for divorce, he has continued to try to control the proceedings by throwing things in the way of wrapping it up — like saying, "It's the holidays, let's not ruin Christmas with finalizing things." Now, he wants paternity testing before finalizing. This divorce should have taken only a few months, but we are now on month eight."

"Emotional abuse is real. Emails, texts, etc., should be looked at as evidence of emotional abuse. It is very difficult as a professional to file abuse charges over things that are not physical because of what may appear in the public record could potentially be damaging to your reputation."

"Although I have an injunction in place, the officers called to one incident arrested me without looking into the injunction. I kept trying to explain and that he was at my residence and we did not live together."

"My ex-husband continues to stalk me and create negative situations, which hurt me financially. Examples include turning me in to code enforcement for renovations he made, and calling assessment offices to give false information. He refuses to move forward with a divorce."

"I remained in an abusive relationship against my will, now, for an additional eight years. The opportunity for abuse toward and involving the children was increased by the family court. Only after reassignment of my case did we gain any relief, and it was too little too late. I believe an essential element to this problem is family court judge's power. A clinical social worker custody evaluator, a CASA volunteer and a forensic psychologist all recommended different orders, but our judge was able to rule according to his own whim, as all family court judges may do. That is unacceptable. Shame on family court."

"My husband didn't hit me so I couldn't file abuse charges. But he abused me emotionally and mentally to the point that I have PTSD symptoms. I was afraid of this man. That isn't normal. I'm slowly working through it, and he has limited contact with our daughter. I'm very grateful for that. It's mostly by his choice, though, because he basically didn't want to be bothered with us anymore. It scares me that he may be able to go back and ask for more time."

"At my final divorce hearing, the only thing the judge asked about was custody (I receive no child support.) Fortunately, I had a well-regarded lawyer and that seemed to tamp down the questions. I do think the presumption that an abuser is a perfectly fit parent is a problem, especially with no supervision and no counseling in place for the children. Many prohibitions of what can be said is going to prove highly destructive in the long-run. The law also allows an abuser to drag out the court case for an extremely long time. Finally, my husband is prominent, and nearly everyone from our old life sided with him because fame trumps all. I was totally unprepared to be completely ostracized like that. It has been incredibly painful to have people basically turn their backs on me in public."

"My ex-husband still tries to coerce me into letting him choose where I live, where I shop, where our child goes to school. I have to stand firm in order to not be affected. He will pick up my child and linger in my apartment so he can look around. He will try to look through my trash. It's been six years. It won't end until we no longer share custody. Now, he is telling our child that the amount of time he spends with mom and dad is not fair so my child has been asking me why it isn't fair. What do you say to that? He will always attempt to have control. Counselors tell me I am strong and I see the red flags and I am in control of my life. So, why am I sitting here crying and feeling terrible? Because the system hasn't protected me. It's still an everyday issue."

"The emotional and verbal abuse continues to this day. This is not a person you can have a reasonable discussion in regards to decisions for our child. Anything can set him off. He has embarrassed us publicly at sporting events and school."

"It's an enormous problem — the lack of support in family court for women coming out of abusive relationships. Everyone is assumed to be a good parent. If a mom says her ex is bad for the kids, the judge assumes she's just being spiteful or too fussy. My children are emotionally and psychologically abused every two weeks by their dad. I think he's physically abusive, too, but can't prove it. I continue to take myself and the kids to therapy in hopes it will someday come out, but we've been going for over three years and they haven't told yet. I think he tells them he will kill me if they tell."

"I was a stay-at-home mom with an emotionally abusive husband. We have two daughters. I initiated divorce in 2012, and I was so scared of leaving that I didn't hire a lawyer. I agreed to everything and got myself in a horrible situation that has lasted for the past four years. I took him to court two times trying to prove emotional abuse of the children, to no avail. It is so bad that I ruined a potentially good relationship out of fear of my ex and his threatening to take the children from me. He has ruined this family financially, emotionally and psychologically. I'm unsure of what to do now."

"It's been over seven years and my ex still traumatized me. Since we have children together, I have never been able to find space to heal effectively to deal with him as the parent of my children. He continually wants to dominate and destroy because I ended our marriage."

"My ex got remarried less than a year after our divorce. He uses the new wife to try to manipulate me into doing what he wants. She hasn't caught on yet."

"I do not talk about the abuse. Any minor negative comment made about my ex is met with criticism. I try not to speak negatively about him with my son, but I feel that I must address this type of behavior when it occurs in front of him. His father seems to have no regard for how this affects him. But he never did."

"I was treated like I was the one doing the abuse and he was the victim. I had to repeatedly sit across a table from him. He emotionally abused me right in court and in front of the mediator. Even after witnessing his behavior, they did nothing."

"I feel so lonely. Very few people understand. My ex is singularly focused on me. He uses our children to feed his narcissism and control needs and to continue to torment me. Well-intentioned people make comments like 'He'll lose interest'. This will never happen. Also, he is $13,500 in arrears on child support and has never paid the 50 percent medical bill requirement, but nothing happens to him. Seven years of enduring this is exhausting. He abuses our children, but they are alternately afraid of him and long to have a normal relationship with him. They they wouldn't tell the therapist what was happening. My youngest is 8. I have 10 more years of this."

"There does need to be some sort of awareness on the part of the courts about how the courts abuse the victims. This was an issue when my son was being molested by his stepbrother. My son told me about it. My lawyer said I had to reported to the police. I was terrified. I got rape crisis involved, and I didn't want my son go away on a vacation with them, which was scheduled while this was happening. In the court, where I tried to stop that vacation, but my ex argued that the vacation had been planned. Then the lawyers discussed how I allowed the child to go to my ex's house around the same time as I was reporting the abuse to the police, and wondered why would I have done that if I was really afraid for my son. But if I had tried to keep our son away from my ex on that same day, then I would've been nailed for trying to alienate him. This is a perfect example of how you can't win when trying to do the right thing."

"I really want to see a big change in how the court protects children and the protective parent. I feel constantly abused by ex and I am trying to protect my child, but to do that I am forced into having contact with him, which exposes me to abuse. I get so anxious around him and even having a contact book and separate contact phone causes me anxiety. I don't have any face-to-face contact, but I get scared of even turning the phone on or readying what he has put in the contact book."

"Narcissism needs to be much more closely examined in these situations. My children are suffering and I am being smeared as something that I am not. I have to constantly fight to show how much I love my children. I feel like I am still in the grip of his control. It is hard to heal when he is allowed to dictate so many things in the case because he had the money to file first. His economic status seems to frequently have pull in our case."

96% of responders said their children have witnessed or been victim of the domestic abuse.

CHAPTER 6
CHILDREN OF DOMESTIC ABUSERS

According to the National Coalition Against Domestic Violence, children raised in homes where there is intimate partner abuse face hardships unlike other children that create lifelong consequences. Abusers do not just abuse their partners and ex-partners, they abuse everyone in their family, creating instability and fear. Abusers use unhealthy means to solve all their relationship issues. Children are very vulnerable to an abusive parent, and are in harm's way of all forms of intimate family abuse. An abuser can't just flip a switch and provide a stable environment for their children that they couldn't with their partner. If they could, they would not have become an abuser in the first place.

The consequences of child abuse cost society billions of dollars, according to the Centers for Disease Control. In order for a child to grow up in a healthy, safe and stable environment, the CDC has created the "Essentials for Childhood" program to help raise awareness in understanding what children need. Let's hear some the responders about their experience:

> "My son was 4 months old and in my arms during the one-time physical abuse; he was not harmed and did not need any trauma therapy due to his age."

> "One of my children hasn't seen his dad for three years. He finally had to see him, and was choked. CPS and the judge dismissed a statement by a known domestic abuse expert, who documented the abuse. The judge is putting my son in reconciliation therapy to see his father again."

> "My ex-husband only sees our child 40 days per year, assuming he is in the country and wants custody. He has rejected many of his custody weekends by refusing to pick up or allow drop-off. I wish there was a way to terminate

parental rights based on lack of parenting visitation."

"[My ex-partner] kicked me out of the house because I was 'being irrational and to think things over for a few days' and refused to allow me to take our 5-month-old daughter with me."

"I left a highly toxic, verbally and emotionally abusive relationship when my child was only 3 months old. We were not married but lived together. I was immediately dragged into court. He lied about his involvement with our child. The judge deviated from the Arizona state guidelines for such a young child and awarded 50/50 custody on a rotating two-day schedule and allowed my ex to immediately take my son, who had never been away from me for more than a few hours, on a four-day trip across the country."

"I have been through the family court system for three years now; my children are only 3 and 5 years old. I left my abusive ex-partner when my children were 3 weeks and 2 years old. I waited until my ex-partner was asleep, and we left in the night with nothing. I went to my mum's, thinking I was escaping him and the abuse, but that is when the abuse and violence got a lot worse for me and my children. He then started a custody battle for the kids. He told me he did not want or care for me when I lived with him. I am still in this battle; it seems will never end. My kids won't sleep in their own beds. They are clingy and won't let me out of their site. They cry. They want to stay with mummy. It is heartbreaking."

"When our child disclosed abuse, the person who abused him got more custodial time. Now, he is afraid to speak out. He was abused again and nothing was done. This is not the lesson we want to be teaching our children. He is only 9."

"The family court system is being used as an ongoing tool of abuse and manipulation; it's a crying shame that my son has suffered through a miserably fragmented "no home" type of childhood and even now, at almost 17, he STILL has no say in the custody schedule.

"In my case, our abuser has abused our child. Our child keeps telling the authorities about it, but the court system keeps putting her back in harm's way. There are legal documents showing his abuse, and yet he somehow continues to get away with it. How do the courts expect these children to grow up and not be abusers themselves? Please help stop the cycle of abuse and remove the children from the situation completely."

70% of responders said they have been financially abused by their abuser.

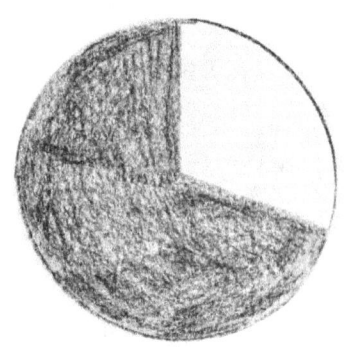

CHAPTER 7
FINANCIAL ABUSE USING FAMILY COURT

According to the National Coalition Against Domestic Violence, nearly all victims of domestic abuse are also abused financially by the perpetrators. The principles of the United States democracy are based on the notion that all people have the right to freedom, even partners in a union. But our laws tie the financial decisions made by only one spouse to another. This practice gives abusers a free and often legal way to have power and control over their victims. Abusers often go further in harming their victims by intentionally causing financial hardship in order to keep their victims in fear of the abuser.

Using fear and threats, the abuser can then control the decisions of the victims, which is the ultimate goal. While an abuser may not have the same access to a partner's finances after divorce, an abuser can still cause serious financial hardships through a number of means after divorce. Even the threats of financial hardship can cause enough fear in their victims to achieve the goal of control for the abuser. In recent years, in part because of changing social norms regarding gender-based custody, family court is becoming the preferred arena for abusers to create fear and instability in their victims' lives simply by filing multiple family court actions. Each time an abuser files in family court, the victim is faced with legal fees, court fees, lost wages, anxiety, and fear for their children that can lead to much deeper health issues, requiring expensive treatments. Protective parents are driven to protect their children from the abusive parent and will often spend through all the money they have in legal fees.

Many abusers use child support as a way to hurt and control their victims. Sometimes abusers file for custody just so they don't have to pay child support. Further, male abusers who are statistically at a greater financial advantage over women victims financially, simply because of pay inequalities. When abusers use money as way to abuse, they cause instability in their victims' home-life, which is not good for children. Some abusers even argue that the financial instability, some thing they caused, makes the protective parent's home unfit for children. Here are the words of the victims:

> "My ex manipulated the system to cut my child support in half. I had to pay him $20,000 to keep my home. I should have got better legal advice, but I was

scared of his violent temper."

"I won a relocation case and moved because I was unable to find work for a very long time in my field where I lived. I also lived in one of the most affordable cities. I moved within an hour drive and a hour and a half ferry ride. He has been taking me to court almost once a month. This has caused me to miss work because I have to travel to the other city and has caused me a lot in travel costs and court filing fees. He has lost all applications to vary orders with the exception of child support and to vary the visitation while unemployed. I feel the repeated litigation and harassment is ruining my life and my emotional state, jeopardizing my job and my relationship. The lack of financial support is also causing me to go into a lot of debt to survive."

"I am 55 and was with my ex 27 years. He stole everything. He hired a super lawyer to help him with all his dirty deeds. When the children and I were going to the DV shelter, we packed our personal items. My ex stole everything out of the boxes, replacing with garbage to weigh them down. Our special needs child tried to commit suicide after unpacking her boxes. I don't allow him any access to our children now. He lived in hiding for three years but the foreclosure attorneys found him. I then had him served to finalize the divorce. When I complained about no support, the judge said, 'He isn't going to comply.' I wasn't given any child support in the orders for our minor special needs child."

"I've spent over $30,000 divorcing my abuser because he fought me every inch. I walked away with almost all our debt, two children to raise by myself and have yet to receive any child support. I can see why women stay. It is not easy to leave. And I consider myself lucky because I have a good job."

"I have been homeless for five months, staying with people and in shelters, living out of backpacks with my 13-month-old baby and my older daughter, 13. I am having my case appealed by the family violence appellate project and will never stop fighting for our freedom."

"I was financially and emotionally abused and I feel this pattern has continued. No physical abuse, but I live in fear. I live in fear of being taken to court. It costs me a lot of money I don't have and being abused through the courts is something that needs to be taken more seriously. I am self-represented, and I feel that him taking me to court is a way to continue to abuse me. I tried to get a parenting coordinator and he refused. I currently have a court application for this because it was adjourned. I am also supposed to take him to court to raise support, but I am reluctant."

44% of responders said their children have received some form of trauma treatment therapy.

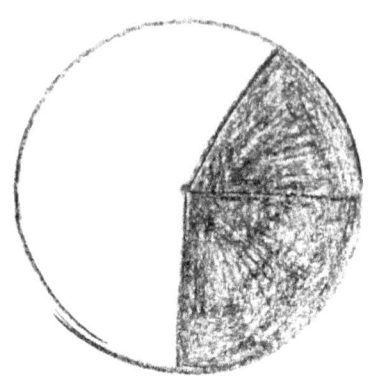

CHAPTER 8
NO TRAUMA TREATMENT

According to the National Coalition Against Domestic Violence, 90 percent of children in homes where there is domestic abuse will witness the abuse. Intimate partner abuse creates fear in the entire household of people, no matter who is hit or the direct target of abuse. Trauma in childhood, left untreated, creates a host of lifelong illnesses and consequences that costs society billions of dollars, according to the Centers for Disease Control. Prevention. Trauma treatment is the key to counter this epidemic and curb the costs for society. Experts in the field and multiple studies have shown that the faster a child can be removed from abuse and their feelings about it validated, the less longterm emotional damage is created. Children, like all victims of any trauma, need to be free of abuse in order to heal from the trauma. Imagine the victim of a car accident having to heal while getting repeated run over through their treatment. It is impossible.

Abusers often stand in the way of trauma treatment because they fear third-party investigation of the circumstances for obvious reasons. One case I learned about in 2015 involved an attorney whose daughters accused him of sexual abuse. The attorney ultimately committed suicide rather than face a jury in the criminal case. In the aftermath, at least one adult in the daughters' lives had a feeling something was wrong because of the girls' public behavior. He went to their father to report his concern and suggest some sort of intervention. Their father, who was of course an the abuser, dismissed the concern and redirected the friend.

Abusers often fight treatment because they don't want to pay for it. They don't see it as important. However, sometimes abusers see ways to use third parties, such as parent coordinators and social workers, as tools they can manipulate to control and discredit their victims. In those case, abusers will often pay for the help.

Other abusers refused family treatment or treatment for the child simple because they enjoy the power of the "veto." Too often, family courts give abusers this power in medical decisions just by giving them 50/50 decision-making, and then the abusers use that power for the sake of it rather than in making decisions that are best for the children.

Here are the experiences relating to trauma treatment shared by the responders of the survey for this book:

"My gosh, there's so much to say, having gone through so much from age 2 to age 18 with my son and my ex. It finally culminated in me having to kick my son out. He was being abusive towards me. He is living with his dad and I don't really even see my son. I have just found a source for trauma counseling; the past 16 years have been really dealing with crises."

"Seven years on, I try and manage the situation as best I can. I still feel my ex is an 'unknown' quantity and that is always on my mind when dealing with custody and co-parenting issues."

"I work for child welfare. I had been to court with these attorneys and the judge several times on deprived cases. My opinion on the safety of a clients' children held weight. When I was fighting for the safety of my own children against their father, suddenly, I was just angry. It was a very disappointing and sobering experience."

"My son is now 15 and has the right to say no to visitation. He has spent two days at his father's in the last two years."

94% of responders believe family court needs reform.

CHAPTER 9
NO SATISFACTION

In 2015, I interviewed a family court judge about the custody dispute process in Florida. I also wanted to know his general views about the process and how he saw his role in the life of the children, who were the center of his cases. I would have liked to speak with him for hours, if not days, but of course, his incredibly busy docket didn't allow for that. I was thankful he gave me 30 minutes and that he answered every question I posed. I was impressed with the care he seemed to have for the topic. Much as been written about family court judges in this book, so far, and not a lot has been positive. I find it understandable. The dynamic of domestic abuse is not universally understood and that can lead to unintended consequences. Victims who share children with their abusers live their lives on life rafts floating in the middle of a giant ocean in the middle of a hurricane. Much of a victims tone is based in an enormous sense of urgency that no one in their vicinity seem to share. Their little rafts loaded with their children is vulnerable and could flip at any second and no one seems to understand what is at stake.

Judges often take the blunt of that frustration and anxiety because in the eyes of the victims, judges have the power to curtail much of an abusers' abuse and calm the waters for the protective parents' journey. Abuse victims often feel helpless and turn to family court judges and other people of authority for help in stopping the abuse. However, it doesn't usually work that way.

The judge I interviewed told me in 2015, that people should know going into to his courtroom that he will not be able to solve their relationship issues. The laws don't work that way and that is not his purpose. Family court is not the place for healing the relationship, he said. I understand what he meant. Family court is not the place to settle every issue and argument of a broken union.

But, I'm not sure he realized that victims are most often not seeking that kind of relief or resolution to every argument, though it might seem that way. Abuse victims just want the abuse to stop, for themselves and for their children. Abusers often tell their victims, as a way to create fear and manipulate, that they are "wrong" or doing the "wrong thing." Victims begin to believe them, even though they may know deep in their souls something doesn't add up. Victims seek validation. They want to know from a third party that they are not crazy. The family courtroom is often the first place victims even disclose they have been abused. Of course, there are exceptions, but most victims of abuse just want permanent safety for themselves and their children.

Here is how the respondents describe their experience with family court and their satisfaction in it:

> "I don't understand how someone can repeatedly manipulate the legal system and shirk responsibility for their actions and abusive behavior without repercussions. I have lost all faith in the legal system and in those who are supposed to exist to protect EVERYONE, the police and medical professionals. 'The system' is set up to favor those who can put on the best show by saying the right things and hiring the right people. Countless women and children are forever affected and very few seem to notice or care. It's a travesty."

> "Our court system is a joke. They do not take emotional/verbal abuse seriously. They don't even take pictures and reports from police seriously. If I take him back to court, the shit will hit the fan more than anyone really understands (except for myself and my son)."

> "No one seems to really care about the truth. My judge actually said she didn't want to hear any further testimony because it's all he-said/she-said, but I had witnesses to the abuse. Our system is so broken and I still feel just as trapped as when I was in the abusive relationship. My abuser has assaulted eight people in two years and no one seems to care."

> "The legal profession is surprisingly ignorant about the dynamic of domestic abuse in so-called high conflict cases. And despite the more sensible public wisdom, that abusers shouldn't be given the right to co-parent, family court is bending backward in ordering both parties to co-parent despite the history of domestic abuse."

> "I am scared to death that this nightmare will never end. How do you display your whole life for the court?"

> "The current joint legal and physical custody arrangement is only interim, but it was made without a proper hearing. The judge admitted she didn't read any documents during our dispute resolution hearing in September, then had only 90 minutes during the following hearing in October. The co-parent, who has repeatedly lied, claimed the investigating social welfare officer was biased against him, and the judge took his words without even asking the officer."

"I know it's still better than what could happen if we go back to court."

"Family court in California offers no protection for children unless there is physical evidence of abuse."

"Oregon grants 50 percent parenting time unless the children are abused, there is drug or alcohol abuse, or there's danger to the children. Cases where the ex is verbally abusive or threatening seem to fall into a crack. If we had never been married, they'd do something, but having been married seems to grant him immunity. The schools also tend to do what's easiest, resulting in harming the kids. It's frustrating. Talking about it paints me as the 'angry ex,' although when he talks about it, it's okay, because 'all women are crazy.' It tears my kids up when he screams or spreads lies about me."

"I was awarded sole physical and legal custody, although despite no contact orders, I'm required to inform him of matters related to legal custody. A guardian ad litem was appointed two months ago and this person was to have provided recommendations on parenting time to the judge. The GAL has yet to even contact me and I assume did not make the deadline. It's unnerving to have people who are not invested in your child's future."

"It would seem that at least in the state of California the system is set up to screw the women out of money, custody. ... 'No-fault' is one thing but poverty and the ability to use a Gavron Warning in a settlement is ridiculous. After all the paperwork, counseling, money spent, it ends up that the follow up to get said paperwork, proof of things, requested documents, is up to each parent? If you could not get this information while married, why would you now? Just because it's on a piece of paper? It feels like there are NO CONSEQUENCES for not following the divorce settlement, and if there are consequences, a parent cannot afford to fight the matters in court, so they are just bullied into same old situation. It's like the divorce was just a motion to go through nothing has really changed!"

"The family court system is child-trafficking."

"The family law system needs to protect victims of abuse and make the abusers either pull their weight in parenting or distance them from it to allow both the victim and children to move on with their lives."

"Abusers are never held responsible for the abuse. A parent tries to leave an abusive relationship to protect the children from growing up around abuse and thinking that it's okay. Then the system puts that child right back into a home with an abusive parent without any protection. This is why domestic violence continues. Why women are scared to report and leave. Something must be done!"

"In my opinion, family courts need to make protection of children's safety their top priority, and stop the 'child needs both parents' assumption when one parent is an abuser."

"I feel the court sympathizes with my ex because he is a veteran. He was mentally ill prior to serving and only got worse. Thankfully, I wasn't the only ex, and I have someone who has shared the same experiences. He is currently on wife number three."

"The court system is painfully slow and the law in Ontario is that one cannot leave the matrimonial home until a childcare arrangement is in place. I also lost a year because I tried a collaborative process, which he just used to play for time."

"Although there is no joint-custody law in Hong Kong – in fact legislators are reluctant to endorse the proposal because of domestic-abuse concerns – joint custody orders have become the sweeping norm in Hong Kong courts. The family court is taking steps even without legislative approval."

"Psychological abuse should be brought into court. I am having trouble living like I used to and making ends meet. The court system only supports men in divorce. My husband has not been sanctioned for not producing documents. No one seems to care."

"The police were extremely unhelpful on a most occasions, some abusive themselves."

"The court system doesn't take into consideration the dynamics of the parents. My attorney at one hearing told the judge everything I do for my children. The judge basically said they only go by where the kids lay their heads at night. What the parent does for the child doesn't play into decisions by the court."

"My ex husband still tries to coerce me into letting him choose where I live, where I shop, where our child goes to school. I have to stand firm in order to not be affected. He will pick up my child and linger in my apartment so he can look around. He will try to look through my trash. It's been six years. It won't end until we no longer share custody. Counselors tell me I am strong and I see the red flags and I am in control of my life. So why am I sitting here, crying and feeling terrible? Because the system hasn't protected me. It's still an everyday issue."

"I have so much to say, but don't even know where to start. I'm sure my story is similar to many others', but my life and that of my children's has been forever altered for the worse, and all I tried to do, when seeking to extricate myself from the situation, was the exact opposite. I just tried to improve my life and that of my children. I feel the effects of this, mourn this, every single day."

"This abuse is not recognized or believed by the court. Father's rights activists have empowered abusive, controlling, narcissistic sociopaths to maintain complete control and continue the cycle of abuse. My children have paid the price and I no longer have a relationship with them because their sick father would not stop using them as weapons. They are too impressionable to see that he is the abusive one. They truly are tragic victims of the broken court system. These are three young people who could have been healthy contributors, but instead today are fragmented because the courts would not allow me to protect them."

"Victims of domestic violence and their children seem to have no support in the courts. We are literally forced to be repeatedly re-traumatized every time we must communicate with our abusive co-parent/former spouse. And we are told co-parenting is best for the kids and that we must soldier on! Essentially, our courts are currently permitting abusers to keep abusing their former partners and to use their children to this end."

"Reform is so necessary, like YESTERDAY. I have been acquainted with several families since my own divorce who have had similar experiences. It is probably the biggest failure of our country that parents are forced to allow their children and themselves to remain victims. This is why we have such an increase in mental illness."

"It is way too difficult to prove emotional and verbal abuse in court. If it was more readily recognized, more women would be protected before things become physical for them and the children. And just because the man (or partner) hasn't 'done anything' to the kids, doesn't mean that witnessing it and then being subjected to ongoing visitation with the abuser won't cause even more psychological harm."

"The justice system has gone too far the other way, trying to make up for the way they treated dads. They don't even look at the real situation and what's best for the children anymore. They are after how many filing fees they can collect. They don't care about people or my kid. I went for help and got re-victimized by the judge and my ex again."

"The California Court of Law is severely lacking competent personnel. Everyone from the judge on down to the recommending mediator are in denial of abuse and its aftereffects. I felt like Alice in Wonderland going down the deep dark hole, landing at the bottom, and I still have not come up for air nine years later. They perpetuate the abuse by keeping the children with the abuser."

"The victim is not allowed to be a victim in courts. We have to be subjected to abuse over and over in the court system, and I am fighting to change this."

CHAPTER 10
HAPPIER STORIES

Though most of the results of the 2015-17 survey for this book showed one heartbreaking tale after another, there were some comments that pointed to happier outcomes, supportive attorneys and officials and other happier stories. However, these were in the minority by far.

Here are the positive comments by the responders:

"Because of my situation, I will complete my degree in forensic psychology. Last month I started employment with our county women's shelter, and plan on working my way up the chain to legal advocate with the shelter."

"I found help here in Chapel Hill, N.C., at The Compass Center. Without them I would not have found the strength in myself to leave the relationship. They saved my children's lives and mine."

"I am so grateful the custody evaluator saw through my ex. The police didn't, but he did. I am just grateful that my kids will be okay."

"I am thankful for my attorney. She was smart and listened. She wasn't perfect, but with her help, we were able to stop my abuser from taking custody of our kids. She agreed to take the case without a retainer, fought for attorney's fees, and won them. She saved my children from a horrible situation."

"I received free trauma treatment therapy for two years, every week, from my local domestic violence center. Without it, I would not have made it through the custody suit filed by my ex-husband years after our divorce."

"Legal Aid provided me with exceptional service and at no charge, regarding my domestic abuse issues. It is very unfortunate that they do not handle custody cases that involve abuse, too. I understand it is a not-for-profit organization and likely does not have the means to handle both. Can't there be another affordable legal advocate for custody cases with domestic violence? My state does not provide any such legal representation."

"It is now my life goal to make changes to keep more children safe from having to go back to an abusive person because of the system. I would like to get involved any way I can."

82% of responders said they initiated the end of the relationship with their abuser.

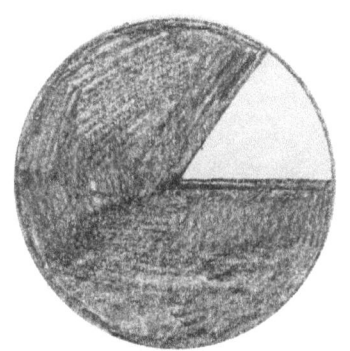

CHAPTER 11
IN CONCLUSION

I am the victim and a survivor of domestic violence. My ex-husband repeatedly abused me in many ways, including physically assaulting me dozens of times. I was ignorant of abuse and didn't understand it. At the time, I really believed that I caused it, or at least played a role in causing my ex-husband to abuse me. I finally decided, 15 years into the relationship, that my ex was the cause of his choice to abuse me. I filed for divorce and full custody of our two young children. He agreed to everything and said he was sorry for what he had done to me and our children. I believed him completely.

I spent the next five years working to keep what I thought was a "good" relationship with the father of my children. I kept him in the loop on every parenting decision and even thought of us as friends. But, the signs were always there, and he was always an abuser. Five years after our uncontested divorce, he blindsided me with a custody suit filled with pages and pages of accusations about my parenting. After an eight-month legal suit, he withdrew his suit and agreed to just a few changes to our original custody order. He had to pay my legal fees and was forced to pay more money for the kids. In every way, it seemed that he had lost his case.

However, I did agree that he should have co-parenting rights on the decisions about the kids. I didn't think that was anything other than proper. I was wrong. He spent the next seven years, until the day our youngest was 18 years old, fighting me on almost every joint parenting decision. He used his power of "veto" as a weapon against me, without regard to our kids. If I thought the kids should play a sport, he would say he didn't. If I wanted to take the kids to my family's for a visit, he would come up with some reason to say no. After years of rarely arguing over our kids, or with me as the primary parent, he suddenly had an opinion on everything and it was most often the opposite of mine. He fought me on everything.

At first, I tried to compromise, but then realized that he wasn't looking for compromise; he was looking for power. So, when I offered a compromise, he would move the goalpost to something else. There never seemed to be agreement. After years of this, I realized that he would fight anything I thought was important. Though I can't speak for him, I can say that he rarely showed happiness about our children, was angry with me often, even over the smallest of issues, and would argue until I completely submitted to his will. If I told him I thought the decision was critical to our children's happiness, or if I thought a decision was harmful to our family, he would not give in. I was backed into one corner after another.

I searched for help from therapists and lawyers. The parent coordinator assigned to our case often told me to compromise, even if the issues were harmful to our children. She gave my ex more credibility as a parent, even though he traveled often, was a documented and admitted physical abuser, and used the court as a way to take back control, and she treated his accusations about me as credible. But, her assessment was not based in evidence or fact. I had written documentation of my ex's abuse. He had attended batterers intervention treatment and anger management. He admitted in family court that he had strangled me while I was nine months pregnant, beat me up five days after major surgery, and all the other abuses, physical and otherwise.

None of his physical abuse was in debate, yet the parent coordinator told me I had to put it aside and move on, even when he continued to verbally threaten me.

The family court system, though we never went to trial after he backed out, looked at us equally, despite his abuse.

There is something wrong with a system when any judge expects the terrorized to be level-headed enough to be excellent parents. I would love to know how a judge reacts when he or she is suffering from abuse. I developed post-traumatic stress disorder from the terrorism inflicted by my ex-husband with the custody suit. I was worried about my children having to live with a man who could choke his pregnant wife. I was worried about how my children would be affected by a childhood of abuse. The parent coordinator seemed to think that fear was unfounded. That was very hard to understand. There are no studies that say domestic violence is healthy for children in any situation. There is no study that says domestic abusers can be good parents. They don't have the necessary skills.

It is completely unnecessary for people to live this way. There are simple solutions: abusers shouldn't never be given parenting rights. Sure, let them have supervised visitation or visitation approved by the protective parent. The only reason that doesn't happen is because judges believe domestic abuse is a marital issue of he-said-she-said. But, there are signs worth noting. For example, unless there is documented wrong-doing to the children, the parent who blindsides the other parent with a custody suit is likely the abuser. I don't know many victims who actively try to prevent their children from spending time with their other parent, despite the abuse. Although I was horribly abused by my ex, I didn't want my kids to be without a father. I remained in denial for a long time and believed that my ex would somehow be able to do with our kids what he didn't do with me: have compassion, love and empathy and put their needs above his own.

I didn't try to keep my kids away from their father. I stepped in when he was abusive, but even then, it was just until he calmed down. Taking away that ability to protect my kids was the worse thing that happened to them. They became the direct victims of abuse after my ex got parenting rights. He still emotionally abuses them, even though they are both now adults.

I know that judges have seen a lot of child abuse and family dysfunction in their time on the bench, but they need to stop conflating the issues with such a cynical view.

I know that society has looked down on "custody-fighting" parents. I have judged them as well. But, here is the problem: two parents don't pick a custody fight. It doesn't work that way. I am shocked that judges seem to forget that a custody battle begins when one parent files against the other. I did not file against my ex. I got a call one day from my attorney, five years after my divorce and the day after I had just spent hours with my ex discussing our children in a completely cordial way. I was shocked to be served with a suit. My ex never told me he was filing or accused me of the things he did in the suit. He never offered any proof of the accusations he made. After eight months, he just dropped it.

Why was I considered as complicit as my ex? I tried offering him many compromises in an effort to stop the suit over those months. He said no to them all. Yet, I was seen as one of the "bad" parents in a custody fight.

The only way I could have stopped it was to agree to everything he wanted, even though I didn't think it was best for our children. I am begging the family court judges and parent coordinators out there to understand that most "ugly custody battles" are not made up of two careless, unhealthy parents. Too often, an ugly custody battle is the result of an abuser using the courts and family law to abuse their victim all over again, as these respondents' comments illustrate:

> "My children and I deserve to live happy and in peace without the constant threats and abuse of their father, but the courts are preventing us to do so by forcing me to co-parent with an abuser who can't be stopped even by the police."

> "If a man abuses a woman and admits to that abuse, then he should never, ever be granted 50 percent custody."

> "Everyone takes their own path and their own time to realize what is happening to them is abusive or domestic violence. Once the realization sets in, it is absolutely imperative that parents take the necessary steps to protect yourself and your children. It's hard and painful and traumatizing, but in the end, only you can advocate for the safety and well-being of your children."

> "Don't give up hope and you will get through it! You are not alone!"

> "I love almost every other aspect of my life, but every time there is a flare-up with him I plunge into a depression. I fantasize about suicide (though I would never do it), and fully sympathize with people who are bullied and kill themselves. I get it. My daughter is my dream come true and the closest person to me, but I seriously contemplate giving her up and moving away. I feel SO alone and unsupported. We live in a small town as mutual acquaintances turn a blind eye, categorizing the abuse as my baby daddy 'drama.' Such an insidiously, dismissive word. I do have friends and family and a wonderful boyfriend who know the truth, but they, like me, are powerless. I truly thought I was escaping a bad situation when I finally left, but I wasn't. I'm still in an abusive relationship. The court rejected my restraining order because he's 'only' been violent once since I left him, even though it was in front of our daughter and in public. He immediately partnered with a strong-minded successful business woman (who shares his sociopathic and narcissistic behavior), and they are prosperous and respected by some in the community. They've also been in court multiple times with different people due to their lack of integrity. But overall, they are successful while I am still struggling. I learned recently about 'learned helplessness,' a psychological condition. It applies perfectly to my situation here and to many other women's, I'm sure. I've tried so hard to get my life together and be a good mom and make the right decisions, but he wins, time and time again, and he beats me back down."

> "I was forced to leave my abuser and finally face how abused I was after

he was arrested and I entered a battered shelter."

"It seems the court wants to be fair instead of doing what is best for the children.
I want my child to have a relationship with their father. I am just not sure at what cost to their emotional well-being."

"Abusers should not be allowed to have unsupervised access to their children and victims should not be forced to 'co-parent' with their abuser. Studies show over and over again that abusers do NOT make good parents."

"My ex was abusive to my son and stepchildren, along with myself. I left many times with the court ordering him to anger management and parenting classes. He took each five or six times. After he would complete the classes, they would give him unsupervised visitation and I'd return. I would have never sent my son by himself. He would scream and cry not to go. I waited until he was old enough that the court would give him a say in what happen."

"Had I known I wouldn't be able to protect my child or continued to be abused, in not just physical ways, but also by coercive manipulative ways, I would've stayed with him. I would have sacrificed myself to be able to raise my child without him using my child's childhood as a way to torment me. Sad but true."

"I think we need to hold a parent who lies and manipulates children against the other parent accountable for their actions. No one seems to understand the devastation emotional abuse causes to all involved."

"I am from Australia. We also have the same issues with regard to the American family law division and the same unfair treatment of domestic violence victims/survivors."

"I had to get out of my violent relationship with my ex-partner. He was abusing me and my daughter, who is not his, and to a lesser degree my son, who also does belong to him. I had to get myself and my daughter out and that meant leaving my son with my ex-partner because he threatened right through the relationship that if we broke up, he was taking my son. He knew this would hurt me the most and end any argument. I broke up with him 18 months ago and he has retained custody of my son only allowing me minimal contact with him. One weekend, three months ago, on my son's birthday, he presented me with a 'Parenting Plan' that I refused to sign on the spot and asked for some time to review it and make my own notes. Two days after giving me the plan, he contacted me to tell me he moved to a town an hour away from my home and had taken my son and enrolled him in a new school, all without prior consultation with me. The very next day I reported the abuse and started court proceedings to regain custody of my son. My abuser now lives with my daughter's father who refuses to see him for who he is, and insists on putting my daughter in danger by requesting to have her (I have had sole custody of her since she was three months old; she is now 11)."

"Litigation began when my ex bypassed mediation to get the parenting schedule he wanted through temporary orders. Rather than keeping status quo for the temporary schedule until we could engage in the process of mediation, he filed a motion, the same week we were exchanging names of mediators. My situation is mild compared to some, I know, but the PTSD I experience means my body can't tell the difference. After an expensive and exhausting battle for 50/50 custody, he promptly found a new girlfriend and has been turning parenting time and responsibilities over to her."

"My son would be 30 now, and this court case happened when he was 14. I thought things had changed over the years, but with my son's recent death, I see things are sadly pretty much the same. Family court reform is huge. I have started to speak out and so often, women in a domestic violence situations say 'he's never hit me, so it's okay.' I would love to find a way to help."

"I spent nearly a year defending myself against all sorts of false allegations, fighting against motion after motion to reach a final parenting plan, which is a 2-2-3 rotation, and is extremely difficult on my 2-year-old because he is constantly being shuffled between homes. My son has no consistency and has recently started showing signs of anxiety, yet I am constantly told it is not severe enough to warrant any changes in the parenting plan."

"My ex has continued to drag me to court to lower his child support, files frivolous motions, and has even attempted to subpoena my bank records to track my spending and where I am going. He bashes me constantly on Facebook and has asked his friends and family members to report back to him on my whereabouts."

"I am on my fourth judge in under two years of constant litigation and have had to have a parenting coordinator appointed. He has refused to pay the attorney's fees I was awarded and due to his position as a vice president, he blocked my attempts to garnish his wages. No one is being held accountable for their involvement and I am constantly feeling bullied."

"I did find an online support group that helps me not feel so alone, but it is disheartening to hear so many people going through what I do."

"My ex is a sociopath and manipulates social workers, attorneys, evaluators, etc. Obviously, these people need more training to be able to identify when they are being manipulated."

"There should be education about domestic violence in high school and how to handle the situation. Also, there should be more legal rights for people leaving their abuser and for the children that were abused or witnessed the abuse. Abusers lie and think nothing they did was wrong. The abuse will continue whether it's to the unprotected child, other family members, or a new relationship. A mother trying to do the right thing should not have to have their child taken away, and the constant fear of getting that phone call saying their child is dead."

"I am forced to share legal custody and unsupervised overnight weekend/holiday visitation with my abusive, alcoholic, mentally ill ex-husband. I was so deeply traumatized by my re-abuse in the family court, that I have avoided even thinking about it because I believe I have some form of PTSD from all I have gone through. I cannot even drive by the courthouse without feeling ill. I fear for my 2-year-old daughter's safety every second that she is with him."

"By allowing abusers to co-parent, the system gives them a chance to continue to abuse the other parents (usually mothers) and the children. Child custody isn't about what is the best interest of children, but about parental rights. It boils down to the patriarchy bias, that children should have fathers at any cost, even when they are abusive."

"We have not begun to have an honest discussion of domestic abuse in this country. And the legal process and legal rules abuse the victim's all over again."

"I wish the courts would better understand Borderline and Narcissistic Personality Disorders to recognize the lies and abuse before them. Children should not be used as pawns for revenge."

"The laws should be followed. If a parent is found guilty of domestic violence, legal custody should not be granted. Judges need to stop using creative interpretations. Domestic violence needs to be taken more seriously in the family court system."

"Reform is very much needed. Persons with degrees in psychology need to be involved in abusive divorces. The legal world is clueless as to the effects of their choices and frankly, from what I have seen, they don't care. It's a man's world. Fighting domestic cases, they make sure we know it."

"There needs to be more awareness around non-physical forms of abuse and coercive control in family court. There is really very little protection until or unless someone is physically injured. People talk about needing to leave and get out before things get physical, but no one really talks about what happens after you leave. I have had people tell me that I need to get over it, he never beat me so it couldn't be that bad. I left because I didn't want my son to grow up witnessing what was going on in our home and how his dad was treating me and thinking that was OK, but it has continued and only gotten much, much worse."

"For many years, I did not realize or admit to myself that I have suffered abuse. I still haven't told anyone in my family. The fallout of my marriage and the way I have been treated by my ex has almost destroyed me."

"The primary reason I stayed with my ex for so long was because he threatened to take my son away from me, and I was worried what would happen if I wasn't there to protect him. When I finally managed to get the two of us away, people told me that my worry was unfounded. But after ignoring my son completely during his first few visits, his father suddenly filed for custody. The guardian ad-litem who was appointed showed an immediate preference for my ex, and recommended he be given custody. My attorney spoke to her and managed to get her to interview us both one more time, and –merely because she caught my ex in a lie – decided I should be awarded custody. The custody battle took almost two years, and then he fought to deprive me of all financial assets. In the end, knowing I had done the best I could to keep my son safe, I agreed to the bare minimum of a financial arrangement just to be done with him. To this day, he still uses money to try to control me, promising to buy things for my son, and then throwing huge fits whenever I ask if he has done this. He accuses me of painting him in a bad light even though I seldom speak of him at all. He is my son's father, after all, and I'd try to spare his reputation for that fact alone."

"It's been my experience through many, many times in court that the judge is stuck in a mindset of 'the children need both parents equally.' While I agree if it's a healthy relationship, that's true, when there is so much obvious abuse happening, it isn't. The courts need to look at each case individually and make a solid determination. 'A son needs his father' was repeated over and over in my case. What was ignored was the false allegations of abuse, the documented emails and text messages, the letters from the school that stated he was interfering with my son's education, and the letter from his friend's mom that stated the abuse she witnessed at the hands of his father. And now my son has not graduated high school, is involved in drugs, and was recently arrested."

"I am tired of feeling or being seen as uncooperative. Like I need to move on, that the abuse didn't happen and he has 'changed.' In two cases, the court granted me a personal protection order against him. He even told the court I belonged to him and I can't divorce him. I don't understand and I feel the abuse is just as bad when I was married. Sometimes, I wonder if it was best that I divorced him, because I fear I am going to lose my children."

"Wish I would have seen and/or admitted the emotional, mental, financial, and physical abuse earlier. I was in denial for a long time. Should have made recordings and videos for evidence and proof."

"When we stop treating children like property of a parent, and actually treat them like people and really look at who is a parent – only then do we have a chance to fix the problem. Because emotional abuse is real and very deep, and these abusers find ways to look like the good guy and continue their reign of terror."

"This is a worldwide problem and very problematic in Scandinavia, where even the UN Human Rights Commission is critical of the rulings of our family courts."

"Children are caught in the middle of these situations too often and need help to find their voice. I would like to help if I can."

"Judges and law enforcement are not educated regarding the depth of damage and abuse towards kids and the victim. Narcissistic abusers know how to control the situation. Even my family couldn't believe it until l told them the whole story about my abuse."

"Thank you for writing this. Some major changes need to happen. I have committed my life to mine and my children's freedom and well-being, and to seeing others gain the same. I won't stop until that happens."

Dear Family Court Judge

THE SURVEYS

The first survey has been circulated since 2015. The Survey was distributed through social media and experts in the field of domestic abuse.
The Surveys were created using Google forms.
The second survey, which quizzed children of family court, has been circulated since 2017.
For information about the surveys, please email julieboydcole@gmail.com

The results of the 2015 survey of victims co-parenting with their abuser:

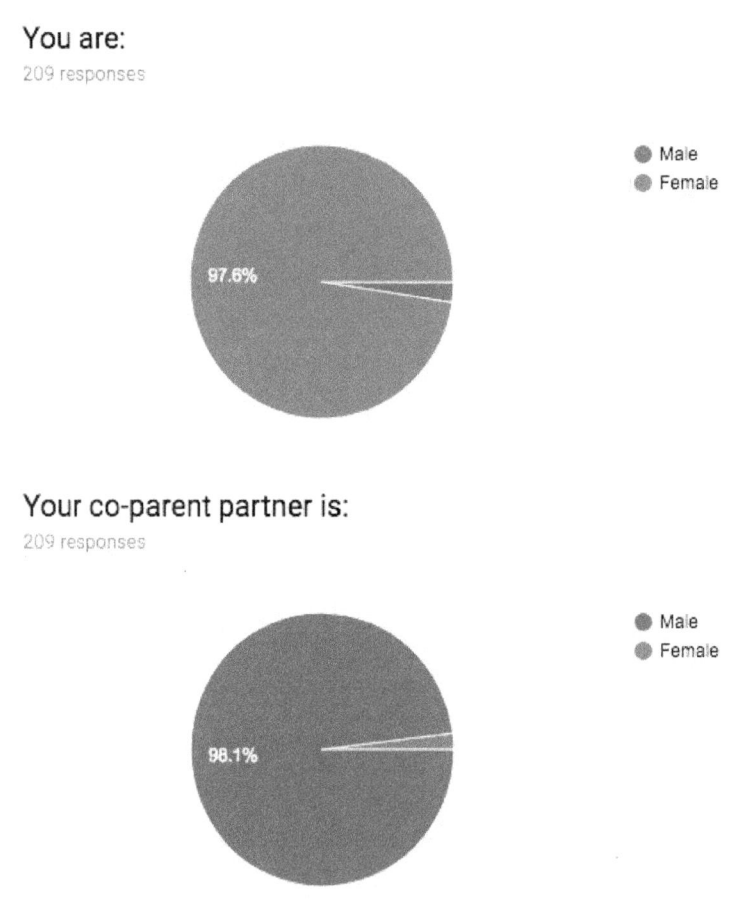

You were the victim of domestic abuse by the hands of your co-parent partner:

209 responses

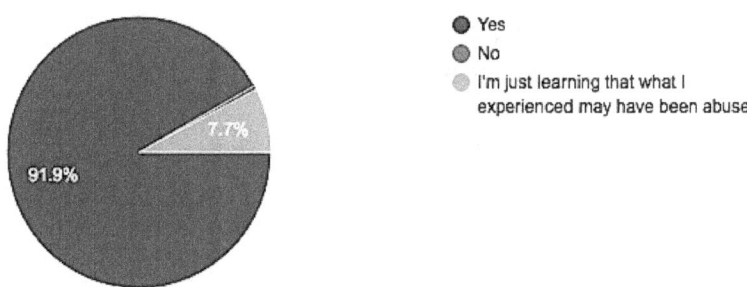

Were you or are you still married to your co-parent partner?

207 responses

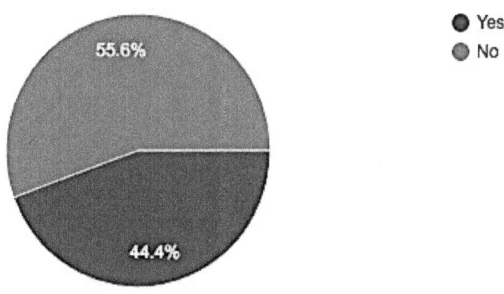

Are you/did you share the same home?

206 responses

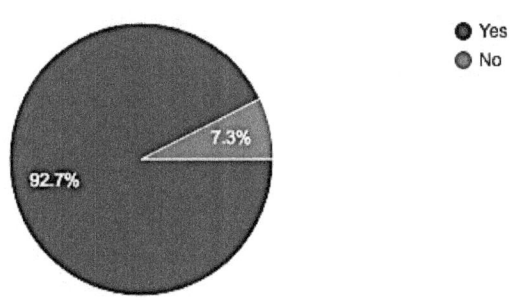

Have you ended this intimate relationship?
207 responses

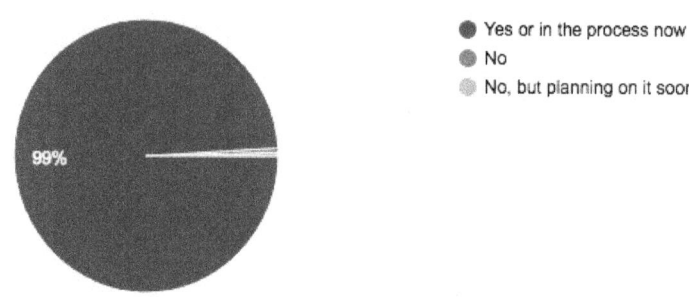

- Yes or in the process now
- No
- No, but planning on it soon

99%

How many children do you share?
207 responses

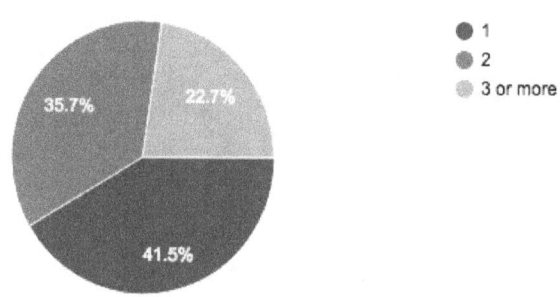

- 1
- 2
- 3 or more

35.7% 22.7% 41.5%

Who is seeking/sought the end of the relationship?
205 responses

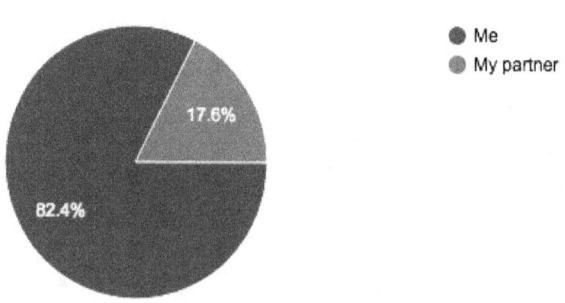

- Me
- My partner

17.6% 82.4%

Do you share physical custody of your children?
202 responses

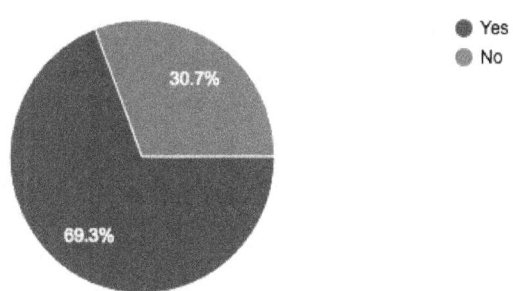

- Yes
- No

30.7%
69.3%

If yes, how many nights a month does your co-parent partner have physical custody of your children?
174 responses

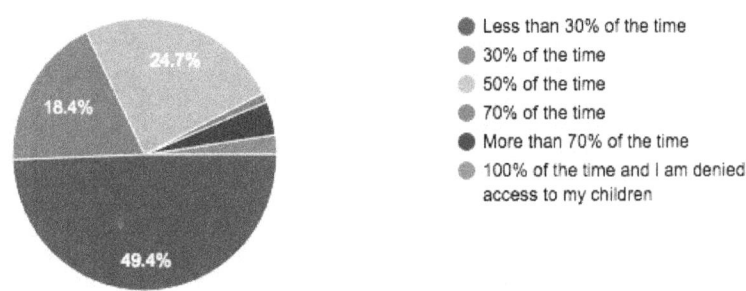

- Less than 30% of the time
- 30% of the time
- 50% of the time
- 70% of the time
- More than 70% of the time
- 100% of the time and I am denied access to my children

24.7%
18.4%
49.4%

Has your original custody agreement been changed by court action since your divorce?
201 responses

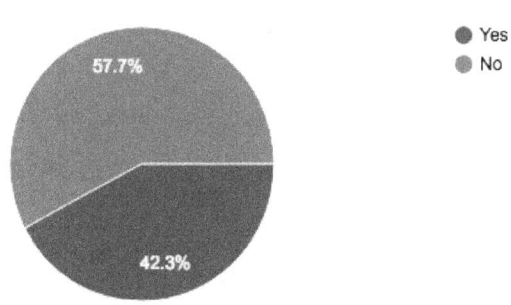

- Yes
- No

57.7%
42.3%

If yes, did your co-parent partner seek a change in the custody agreement by court action?

156 responses

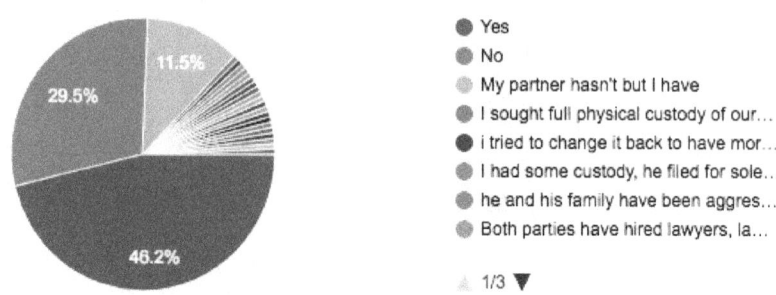

Was domestic abuse presented by you as evidence in your divorce or custody matters.

199 responses

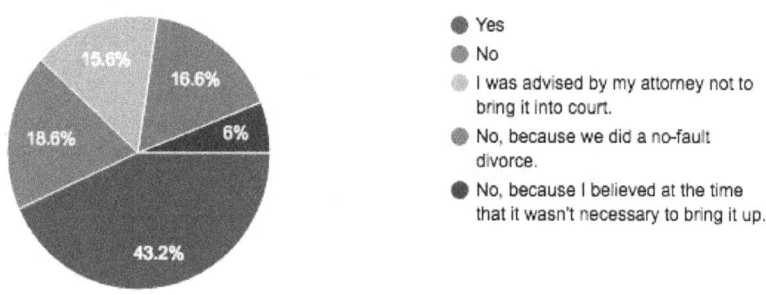

If yes, did any authority investigate the circumstance of the abuse or allow testimony or evidence on the abuse?

138 responses

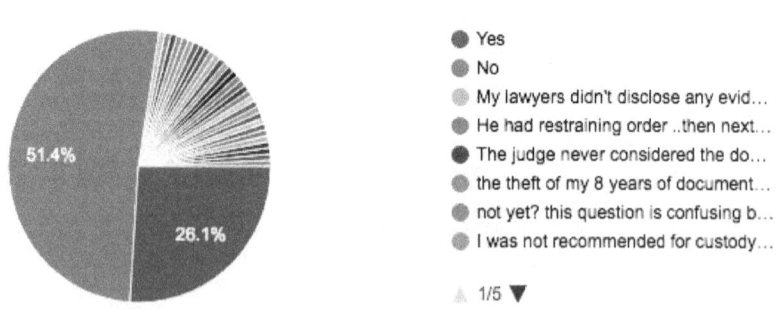

If you are separated/divorced from your abusive partner, are you still being abused by this partner?
203 responses

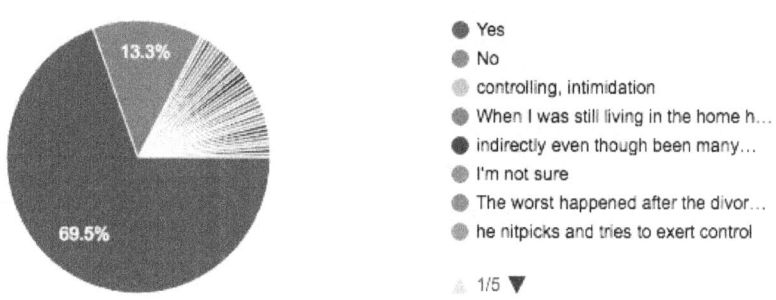

- Yes
- No
- controlling, intimidation
- When I was still living in the home h...
- indirectly even though been many...
- I'm not sure
- The worst happened after the divor...
- he nitpicks and tries to exert control

1/5 ▼

Are you receiving any trauma therapy counseling?
206 responses

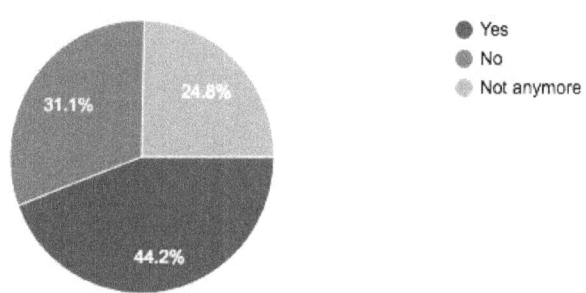

- Yes
- No
- Not anymore

Has your child witnessed or been the direct victim of any physical, emotional, financial or psychological a... the actions of your co-parent partner?
207 responses

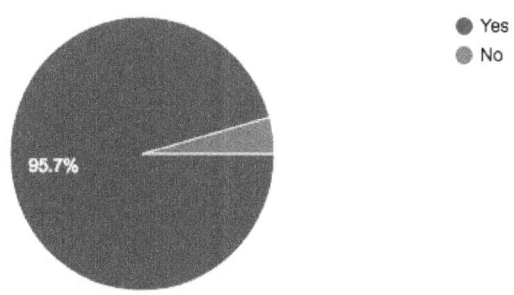

- Yes
- No

Is your child receiving trauma therapy counseling?
205 responses

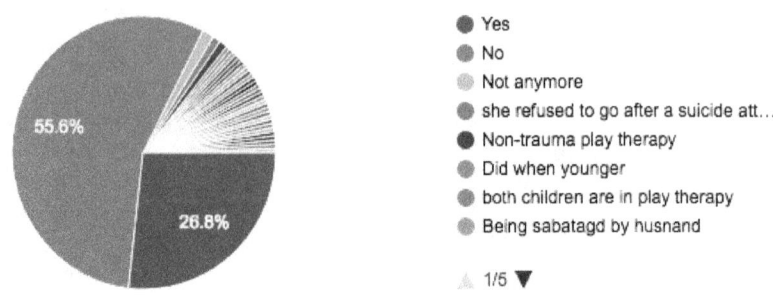

- Yes
- No
- Not anymore
- she refused to go after a suicide att...
- Non-trauma play therapy
- Did when younger
- both children are in play therapy
- Being sabatagd by husnand

1/5 ▼

- 55.6%
- 26.8%

Are you satisfied with how the legal system treated your case?
198 responses

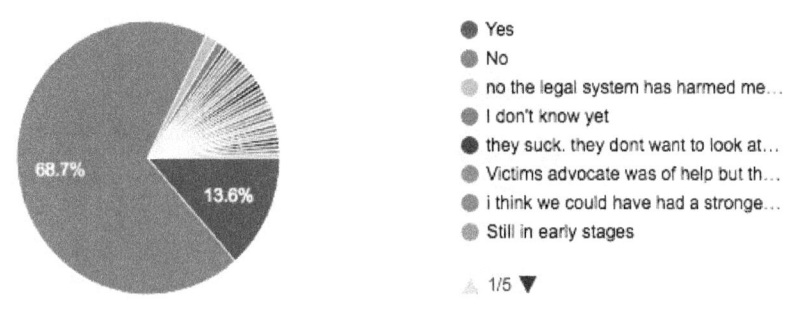

- Yes
- No
- no the legal system has harmed me...
- I don't know yet
- they suck. they dont want to look at...
- Victims advocate was of help but th...
- i think we could have had a stronge...
- Still in early stages

1/5 ▼

- 68.7%
- 13.6%

Are you satisfied with the custody arrangement?
198 responses

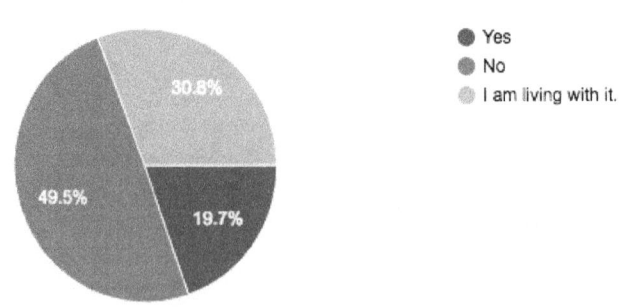

- Yes
- No
- I am living with it.

- 30.8%
- 49.5%
- 19.7%

Do you think reform is need in the standards of family court?
193 responses

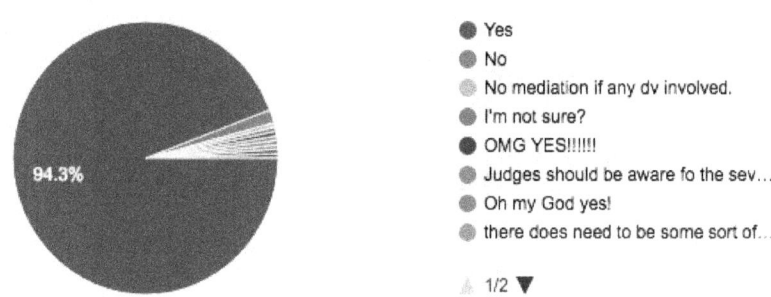

What year did your court case first begin?
177 responses

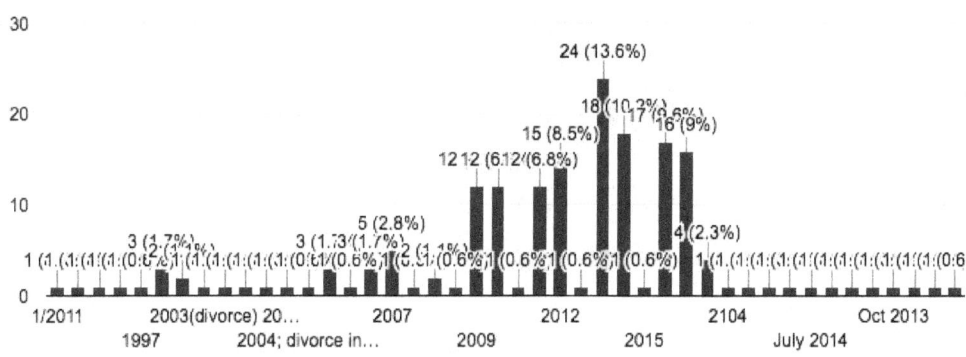

The results of the 2017 survey of children of a contested custody case:

Your age
18 responses

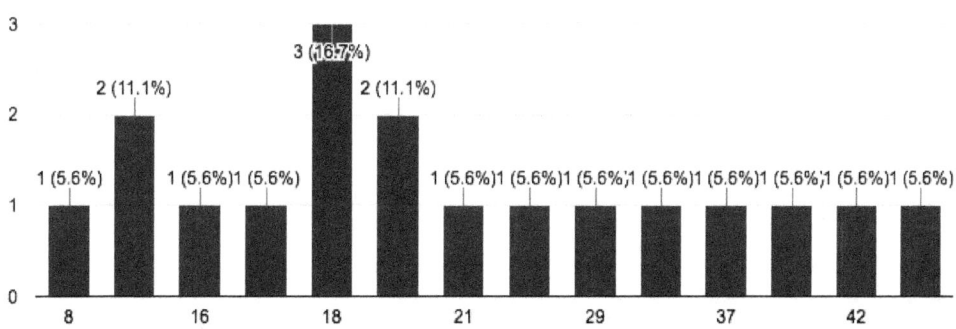

Are you male or female?
18 responses

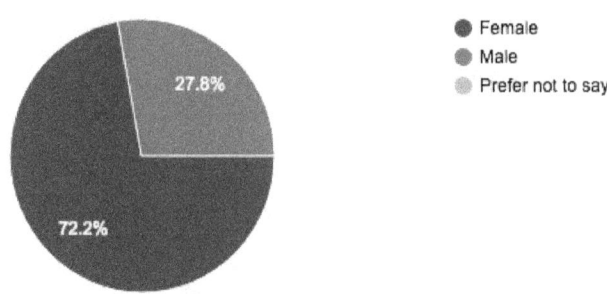

Do you have siblings?
18 responses

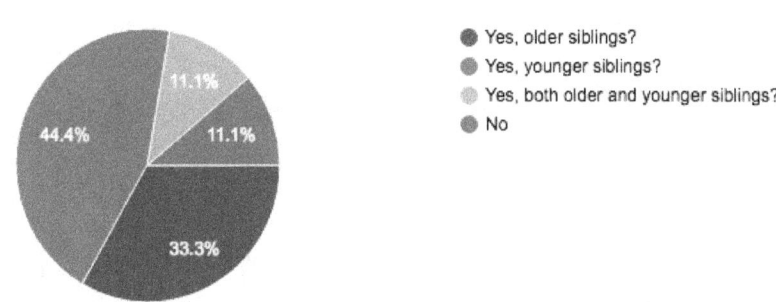

Were you a child in a custody dispute between your parents/grandparents/caregivers?
18 responses

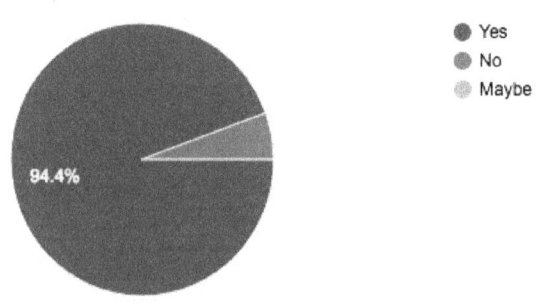

At what age were you when you first learned there was legal action involving your custody?
17 responses

- Less than 5
- Between 6-9
- Between 9-12
- Between 13-17
- After I became an adult, I found out that there had been a custody dispute about me.

Did a judge decide your custody?
17 responses

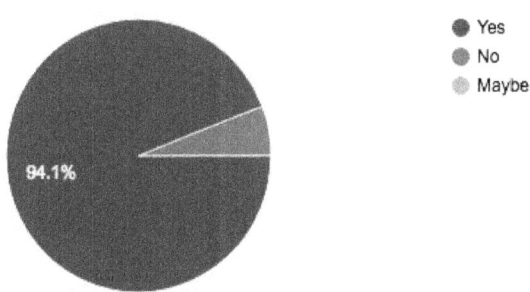

- Yes
- No
- Maybe

Was there domestic abuse in your childhood home?
18 responses

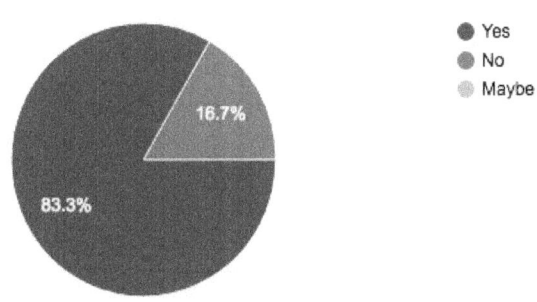

- Yes
- No
- Maybe

Who was the primary abuser?
16 responses

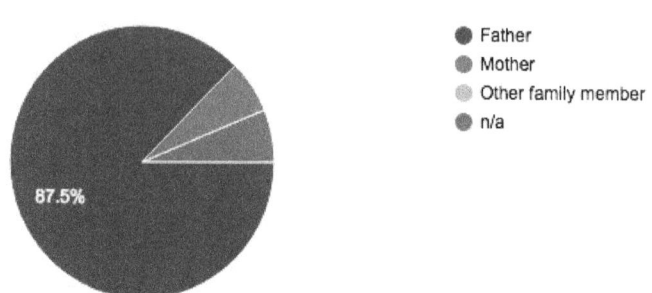

On a scale of 0 to 5, please rank the stress you felt during your childhood? With 0 being no stress and 5 being nearly daily stress?
18 responses

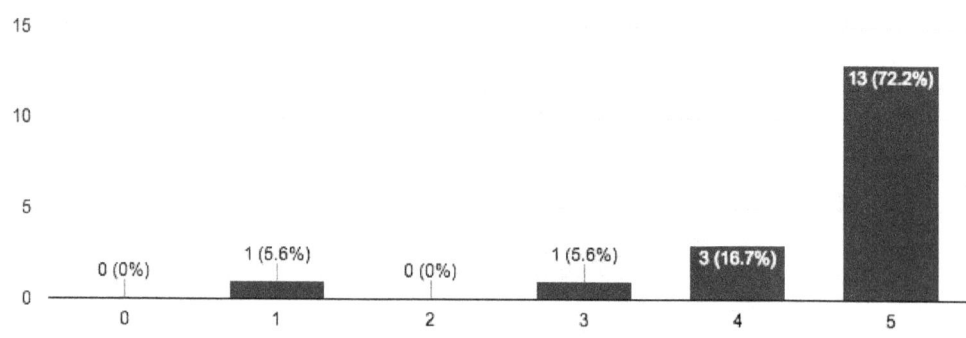

On a scale of 0 to 5, please rank the stress you felt while the legal action was underway.
17 responses

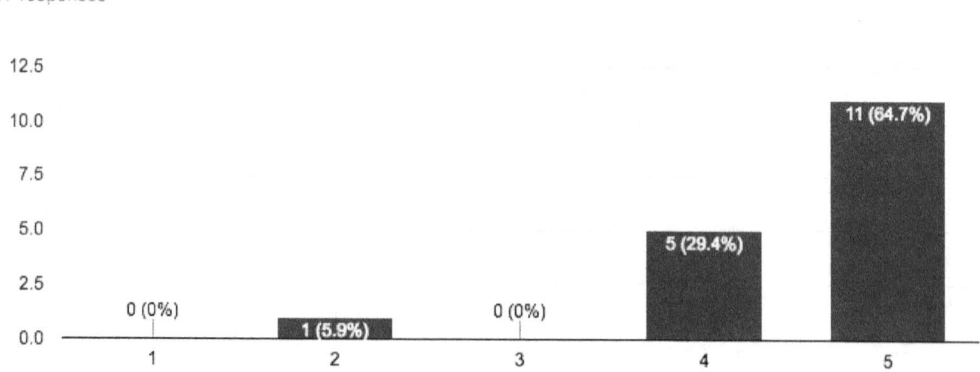

After the legal action was over, did you feel better, worse or the same about your custody?

17 responses

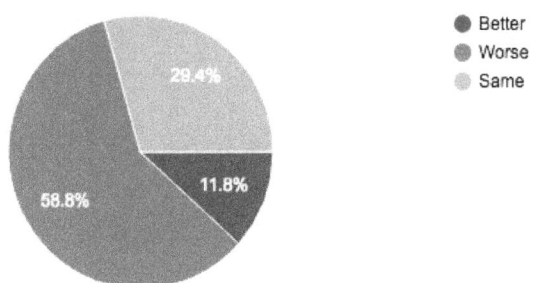

- Better
- Worse
- Same

58.8% / 29.4% / 11.8%

Did you feel a part of the legal action or did you feel that decisions were made without your input?

17 responses

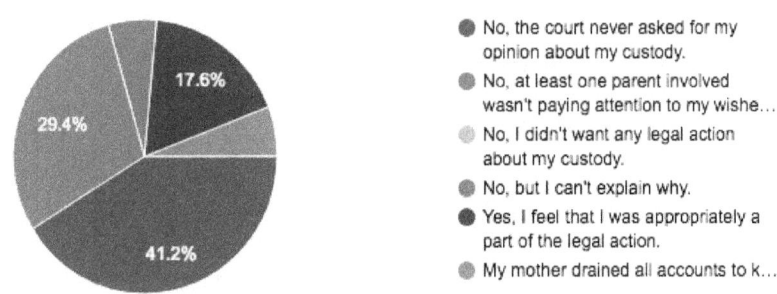

- No, the court never asked for my opinion about my custody.
- No, at least one parent involved wasn't paying attention to my wishe...
- No, I didn't want any legal action about my custody.
- No, but I can't explain why.
- Yes, I feel that I was appropriately a part of the legal action.
- My mother drained all accounts to k...

41.2% / 29.4% / 17.6%

Generally, did the custody action ultimately make your life better or worse?

17 responses

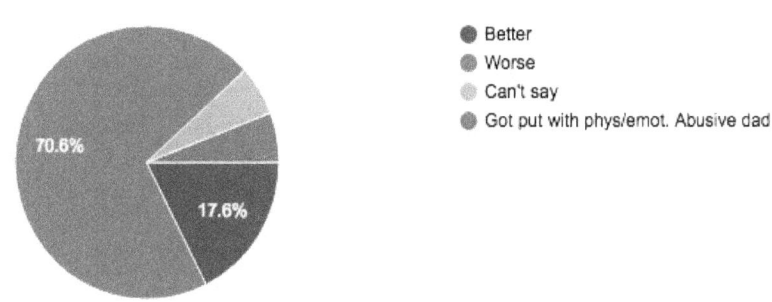

- Better
- Worse
- Can't say
- Got put with phys/emot. Abusive dad

70.6% / 17.6%

Were you upset about the custody action?
17 responses

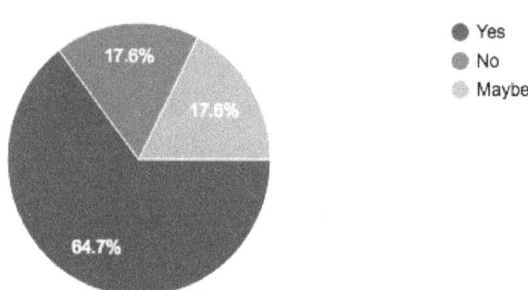

After the legal action regarding your custody, did any of the treatments checked continue? Stop?
16 responses

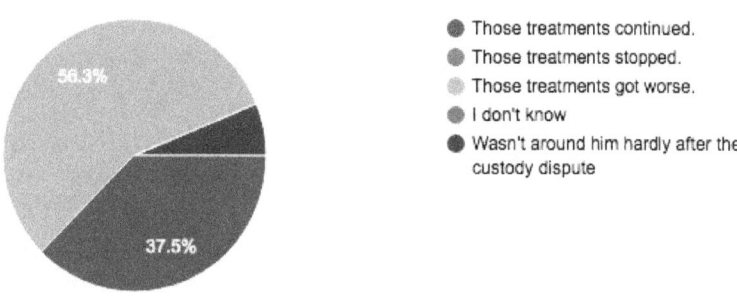

After the custody action, did your childhood improve?
17 responses

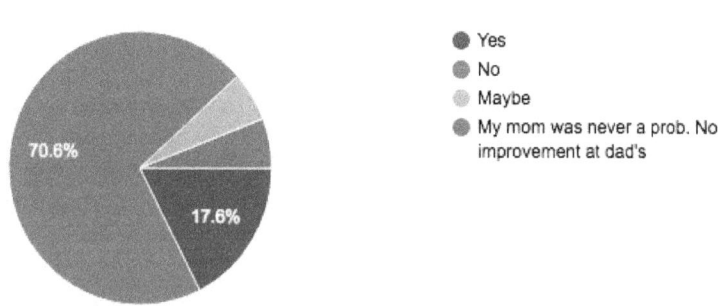

Were you happy with the custody action?
17 responses

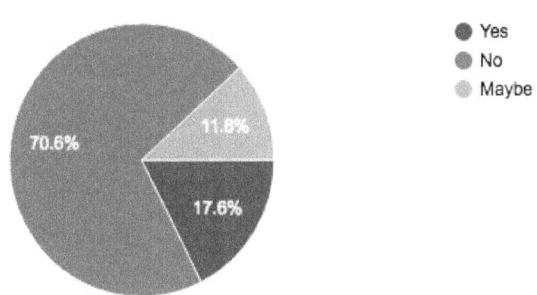

- Yes
- No
- Maybe

70.6%
11.8%
17.6%

Were you happy with the outcome of the custody action?
17 responses

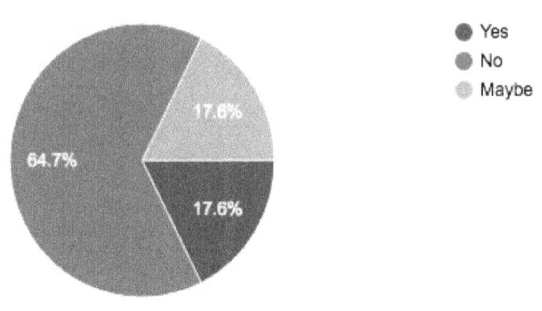

- Yes
- No
- Maybe

64.7%
17.6%
17.6%

Do you think custody of children should be decided in family court?
18 responses

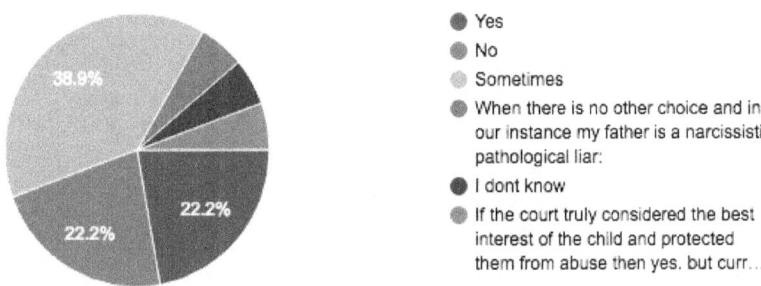

- Yes
- No
- Sometimes
- When there is no other choice and in our instance my father is a narcissistic pathological liar:
- I dont know
- If the court truly considered the best interest of the child and protected them from abuse then yes. but curr...

38.9%
22.2%
22.2%

Do you think family court should be improved/changed to better serve the welfare of children?
18 responses

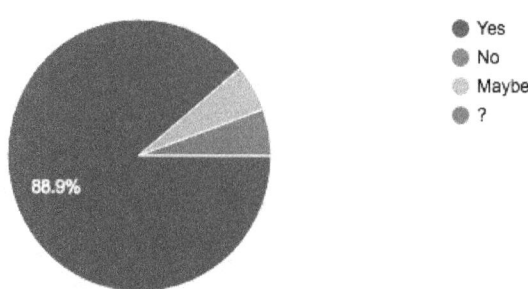

- Yes
- No
- Maybe
- ?

88.9%

If you answered yes, that one of your parents was an abusers, did the custody action end the abuse?
16 responses

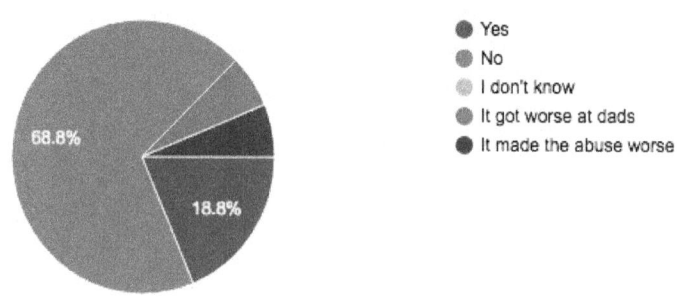

- Yes
- No
- I don't know
- It got worse at dads
- It made the abuse worse

68.8%
18.8%

Did the custody action stabilize your home-life with either parent?
17 responses

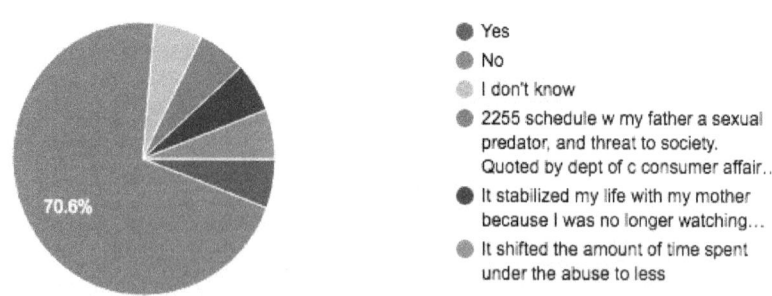

- Yes
- No
- I don't know
- 2255 schedule w my father a sexual predator, and threat to society. Quoted by dept of c consumer affair...
- It stabilized my life with my mother because I was no longer watching...
- It shifted the amount of time spent under the abuse to less

70.6%

Would you say that your home-life was more stable before or after the custody action?

17 responses

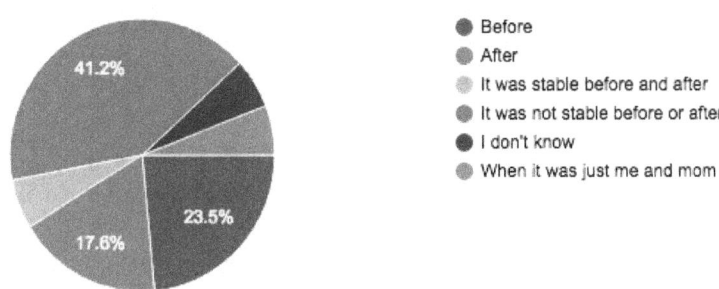

- Before
- After
- It was stable before and after
- It was not stable before or after
- I don't know
- When it was just me and mom

41.2%
23.5%
17.6%

Did you feel there was an adult, parent, caregiver or relative, who you trust would work to understand your needs …? Someone you trusted had your back?

17 responses

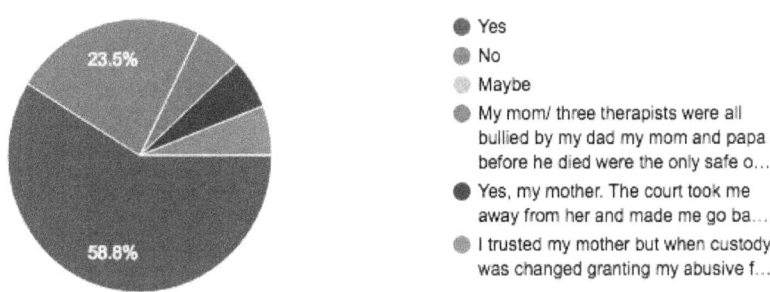

- Yes
- No
- Maybe
- My mom/ three therapists were all bullied by my dad my mom and papa before he died were the only safe o…
- Yes, my mother. The court took me away from her and made me go ba…
- I trusted my mother but when custody was changed granting my abusive f…

23.5%
58.8%

If you answered yes, was that trusted adult involved in the custody action?

15 responses

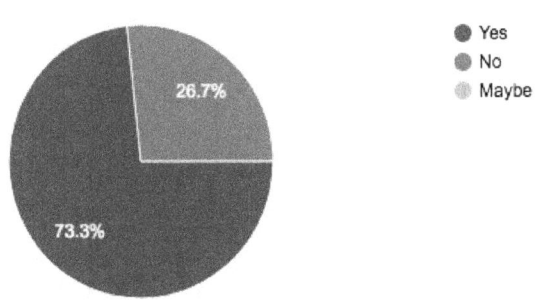

- Yes
- No
- Maybe

26.7%
73.3%

ABOUT THE AUTHOR

Julie Boyd Cole is a mother of two sons, a journalist, writer and business woman. This is her third book and second about domestic abuse. Her first book, *How to Co-Parent with an Abusive Ex and Keep Your Sanity* has been an Amazon best seller for most of the weeks since it was published in 2015.

She has written for the *Miami Herald*, the *Fort Lauderdale Sun Sentinel*, *Yahoo.com*, divorcedmoms.com and the goodmenproject.com among many publications around the country.

Julie is a survivor of domestic violence at the hands of her ex-husband, who was an NFL sportswriter. Today, she is an advocate helping other victims sort through the trauma of domestic abuse.

Julie also writes for bruisedwoman.com and @bruisedwoman on Twitter about the topic of domestic abuse, co-parenting with an abuser and the emotional damage caused by narcissists and personality disorders.

She can be contacted at julieboydcole@gmail.com

www.ingramcontent.com/pod-product-compliance
Lightning Source LLC
Chambersburg PA
CBHW062228220526
45471CB00009B/3395